THE Style STRATEGY

Nina
GARCIA

WITH ILLUSTRATIONS BY

RUBEN
TOLEDO

!t

*it***books**

An Imprint of HarperCollins Publishers

THE Style

tyle

STRATEGY

A LESS-IS-MORE APPROACH TO
STAYING CHIC AND SHOPPING SMART

HarperCollins books may be purchased for educational, business, or sales promotional use. For information, please write: Special Markets Department, HarperCollins Publishers, 10 East 53rd Street, New York, NY 10022.

FIRST EDITION

Book design by Shubhani Sarkar

Library of Congress Cataloging-in-Publication data is available upon request.

ISBN 978-0-06-183401-1

09 10 11 12 13 OV/RRD 10 9 8 7 6 5 4 3 2 1

Buy less, choose well, and mix it all.

VIVIENNE WESTWOOD

Contents

Author's Note

STYLE

I am a working mother and a wife. I am a sister and a daughter. I am a student of fashion and a shopper of everything. Each experience in my life fuels what I do, who I am, and, more important, who I see myself evolving into as tomorrow dawns.

I have goals. For myself, for my son, for my family, and for the people who listen to what I have to say about fashion and style.

Every day I plan, I organize, I schedule, I strategize. And the most important thing I've learned is that while no amount of planning fully prepares one for life's inevitable speed bumps, knowing that I've built a strong foundation enables me to negotiate such bumps with assurance. I must problem-solve at a moment's notice. And sometimes even change course altogether in order to adapt to whatever circumstances are thrown in my path. I have to be quick. I must embrace spontaneity while always keeping my feet on the ground. I must have unwavering trust that I'm making the right decision. If I even begin to doubt myself, I crumble, and nothing gets done. Or rather, nothing gets done correctly.

It is with this goal in mind—of imparting my strategy for achieving this level of self-assurance and confidence, while also economizing—that I decided to write this book. As I look at the women around me—on television, in the news, and throughout the world—I realize that although different circumstances may rule each of our lives, we share the core elements of who we are. We're survivalists. We're nurturers. We're women.

An essential aspect of being a woman is not only taking care of everyone around us, but also taking care of ourselves and each other. We figure out new ways to look and feel gorgeous. Sharing our not-so-secret tips with each other is probably the easiest, and definitely the most fun, way we care for ourselves. As women, it is in our nature to reach for perfection. And although perfection may not be 100 percent possible, getting close is. In fact, I see women getting closer to perfection every day.

I witness this striving toward an aesthetic ideal in the wonderful designs I handle as a fashion director. I see it in pristine garments, astute styling, and impeccable tailoring, among many other examples of the craftsmanship I've come to adore. But I also see perfection embodied in the women walking down my street. Fearless, creative, stylish women who inspire me.

But getting there is a process. It requires a strategy. Taking command of your style and staying chic is but one step in this process—an important one, mind you, but not the only one. Shopping smart and saving our hard-earned money is another very important step. And although it can be a challenge, being practical while honing your style can also be a damn good time. Trust me.

Style is a simple way of saying complicated things.

JEAN COCTEAU

If we ladies are anything, we are resourceful. Long before we earned our own paychecks, we were in charge of stretching pennies for the entire family in order to create and maintain a warm, comfortable home. Through the ages, we've seen it all. No era has been without its crisis. And women have always been a tremendous part of the glue that holds everything together while working through such crises. Our ingenuity and flair for survival has saved the world many times over. But our ability to beautify the world as we save it is what really makes it all worthwhile.

During the Great Wars, through the Great Depression, or, more personally, when we are embarking on a new chapter in our lives, women have always had numerous and seemingly effortless strategies for making ends meet. We always find a way to look fabulous, no matter what the circumstances. Who wore dungarees and kerchiefs with more panache than Rosie the Riveter? The Blue Bell Overall Company, the original name of Wrangler Co., even made a pant called the "Jeanie," specifically marketed to women working in the factories during World War II. These strong American women looked fierce and felt great serving the cause in those custom jeans. It was also during this period, when nylon was in short supply, that women famously drew lines down the backs of their legs in order to simulate stocking seams. Back then, no gal wanted to look unkempt, even while welding the wing of a B-17. Some women even used gravy to color their legs to further the illusion of wearing a pair of stockings. Others used boot polish as mascara. I won't suggest you go this far—I don't advocate wearing food or using shoe polish as makeup. But you have to admire the ingenuity. These women were on a mission to save the world, and they were determined to look good while doing so. These ladies were willing to find any means necessary for making this happen. Their economic situation did not deter them one bit. Nor did the fact that most of the men were away overseas. On the contrary; not having money to spare forced them, like we do today, to find new ways to glam it up without spending a fortune. And glam it up they did: for themselves, for each other, and for morale.

People, even more than things, have to be restored, renewed, revived, reclaimed, and redeemed; never throw anyone out.

OFTEN ATTRIBUTED TO AUDREY HEPBURN

As I write this book, the times again seem daunting. Again, we find ourselves in a global economic crisis. And again, women everywhere are still committed to looking great.

While staying on the cutting edge of the latest trends may be far down the list of priorities for many women right now, it is possible to brilliantly make do with what we have. Owning this skill—and it can be mastered—is worth its weight in gold.

As you have read in my previous books, trends come and go, but real style is timeless. And real style doesn't have to cost money. We all have that friend who wears outfits that you would never have dreamed of putting together. She finds ways to combine the oddest colors with flair, to mix genres, and to effortlessly blend different prints. And she always looks great. Whenever you go out together, she receives so many compliments, each quite often followed with, "You're so lucky—I wish *I* could get away with that!" Well, you can. You don't need to be eccentric and you don't need to be a supermodel to be "that friend." You only need to know how to make the most of what you have, to be creative and truly innovative, and of course, to be confident. And last but definitely not least, you have to know how to shop. Like a pro.

I've always loved fashion and clothes. It's part of who I am, like the color of my eyes or the tone of my voice. And I was lucky enough to grow up with two excellent examples of effortless chic—my parents. But I also had to grow into my own personal style. Life is a style evolution. And I'm still evolving; hopefully, I'll never stop. Every day, designers, models, stylists, friends, books, films, even people on the subway teach me something new. With this book, I will show you how I utilize my appreciation of the style gurus all around us, taking cues from how they wear their clothes and adapting what is truly original into a strategy for the way we shop. I don't believe in dictating what clothes you should buy. Instead, I want to give you the tools to figure out what you want to project to the world and how to own this look.

Once you are able to identify what you love on others, use the expertise that is hidden within us all to reinvent that style into an affordable version that looks great on you. This book is written to help propel you forward, into that place where style and shopping are one. Neither can thrive without the other pulling its proper weight. Effortlessly balancing the two is your mission.

Fashion anticipates, elegance is a state of mind.

OLEG CASSINI

STRATEGY

As soon as I graduated from college, I moved to New York. I was on my own for the first time—in the Big City—and I landed a dream internship handling PR for Marc Jacobs at Perry Ellis. It was thrilling. New York is a spectacular place to start on your path in life. It is so vibrant, and the people who live there are unrivaled in their authenticity. Not to mention, it's one of the fashion capitals of the world, which is important to me for a million reasons. But it can be unforgiving. New York is a tough place for the faint of heart; the city has a way of forcing you to be razor sharp in every way. Living there is hard enough, but thriving there takes a whole different set of sur-

vival skills. And looking beautiful is never just an option. It's a *must*. Even if you don't have a lot of money, personal flair is essential, and New York is the perfect place to learn how to develop that flair on a shoestring budget. There's always something more expensive than what you bought, more extravagant than what you can afford, trendier than what's already yours—there's always something *more*. So you're forced to make choices. Hard choices. You have to learn to be smart and savvy. New York taught me that being chic isn't about the most expensive dress or the latest trend. It's about being *you*.

And being you costs nothing.

The streets of Manhattan are absolutely brimming with style, color, innovation, and creativity. And there I was, in the heart of the fashion industry, working for an up-and-coming designer at a prestigious label. Needless to say, I had to look fabulous. And a starting salary doesn't go very far in New York, no matter what your profession may be. (Let's face it, a starting salary doesn't go very far anywhere anymore.) In those early years, I really began to appreciate all those little tips my mother gave me about taking care of my clothes, applying the idea of self-preservation not just to life, but also to my skirts and jackets, coats and pants. I then took a step toward what I now believe is a style mantra for the real woman: ***Shop smart, stay chic, and make it last.*** My style was (and still is) about making things last forever.

*I love to take things that are
everyday and comforting and make them into
the most luxurious things in the world.*

MARC JACOBS

Back then, I got a crash course in style just being surrounded by so many unbelievably talented designers and amazingly beautiful garments worn by astonishingly gorgeous models. It taught me to appreciate luxury. But it was the real people I saw every day who taught me to appreciate the glamour of innovation and the importance of confidence. Of course, a Prada dress is a work of art—but so is a well-accessorized thrift store find. It's easy to be seduced by all of the glamorous images you see in magazines—I've made a career out of ensuring that's the case—but *knowing* that you are personally rocking your ensemble is invaluable. If you feel good, then you look great, whether you spent $100 or $1,000.

I kept my ears and eyes sharp and focused. I paid attention to everything and I studied all of the stylist's tricks of the trade. I learned from the best how to "fake it" —and to know when faking it *wouldn't* work. I discovered where all the bargains could be found, what consignment shops were guaranteed to have hidden treasures, what store in Chinatown had amazing silk fabric. (And I also learned that if you're going to splurge on anything, make it *shoes*.)

Limitations foster creativity. When you have to make do, you are

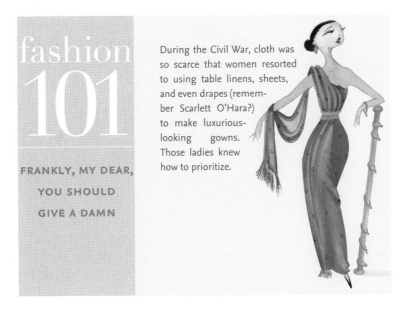

fashion 101

FRANKLY, MY DEAR,
YOU SHOULD
GIVE A DAMN

During the Civil War, cloth was so scarce that women resorted to using table linens, sheets, and even drapes (remember Scarlett O'Hara?) to make luxurious-looking gowns. Those ladies knew how to prioritize.

forced to prioritize and find new ways to make the most of what you have. That's why *Project Runway* is so exciting for me; every season I can't wait to see what these young designers—on a strict budget, in a ridiculously short amount of time, under intense pressure—manage to create. That's where the real magic happens.

One of my favorite fashion anecdotes is about Elsa Schiaparelli, the Italian design genius and contemporary of Coco Chanel, and her first foray into designing. As a young woman traveling through Paris, Elsa was invited to a ball. Being a young student of limited means, she didn't have an appropriate gown. But that didn't stop her—she bought several yards of dark fabric, draped it around herself, and pinned it into place. Her gown looked divine. The pins didn't hold out through the entire evening, and she had to leave early, but she made an entrance, and looked spectacular. And more important, she took a risk and was original. These two essential elements, when properly executed, can result in genius.

By sharing the many amazing tips I've learned throughout the years, I hope that you, too, will make the most of what you have and really embrace the concept of "shopping smart." Although few of us may be invited to a formal ball anytime soon, we can all pretend we're on our way to one. A stylish woman must always look like she's en route to the most marvelous event in her life.

Man cannot discover new oceans
unless he has the courage to lose sight of the shore.

ANDRÉ GIDE

STYLE AND STRATEGY

We all go through times when we are prosperous and times when we simply must economize. In today's society, we've been conditioned to spend without thinking. Trends come and go so quickly that it almost seems as if it's necessary to replace your entire wardrobe three or four times a year just to keep up. It's out of control. We're barraged with so many images of the latest "look" that we lose track of what we actually like—we just know we want *that*. Even when we hate something at first sight (UGGs, anyone?), if the media is so saturated with its image, we will inevitably decide we have to have it after all. It's become more important to find the closet space for our ever-expanding quantity of clothing than to take the time to properly care for what we already own. We see images of celebrities on the red carpet at award shows wearing their gorgeous dresses and fabulous jewels, and we forget that even *they* can't afford what they're wearing.

You don't have to spend a fortune to look fabulous, or sacrifice style when you're on a budget. Less really *is* more. Take stock. Know thyself. Style comes from within. Style is having the confidence to play with fashion, to be creative, to innovate. Again, think *Project Runway*. Your wardrobe is your challenge; use your limitations as an inspiration to see yourself and your clothes with fresh eyes. Be proud of your ability to work it on the cheap.

The *recessionista* has officially replaced the *fashionista*.

fashion
101

WRAPPERS DELIGHT

During the Great Depression, Sears, Roebuck and Co. carried "Sears-ettes," extremely inexpensive wraparound dresses that were reversible (so they required less cleaning) and tied at the side (so the fit was adjustable). Although they were practical, they weren't particularly flattering—think housecoat. Later these frocks were also referred to as "Hooverettes" after the then very unpopular president.

Now, I'm the last one to tell you not to covet great clothes, and I certainly understand the euphoria of slipping into a beautiful new pair of Prada sandals. However, it's time that we all stop, take a deep breath, and learn to appreciate what is already in our closets, proceeding with caution before spending money on something new. It becomes clearer every day that we need to be aware that the Earth's resources are limited and that it is necessary to rein in our disposable lifestyle. We are all sophisticated enough to know that we are part of a community, and that environmental responsibility is ten times hotter than wearing the trendiest label.

My *Style Strategy* is not about doing without; let's be clear on that. It's *not* about feeling deprived. It's about realizing that you can get the same euphoria that Prada gives you by reworking the clothes you already have into a unique expression of your personal style—without sacrificing luxury. I will guide you through the process of rediscovering your wardrobe, seeing it from a new perspective, and learning how to bring it up to date without breaking the bank.

This book will teach you to strategize your shopping excursions by asking yourself the right series of questions.

- Do I already own something like it?
- Can I alter something I already own to look like it?
- Where will I wear it?
- Do I really need it?
- Of course I want THIS dress NOW—but what did I want before I left the house?
- What will I have to forgo later because I spent money on this?

Strategize, and both your style *and* your bank account will come out winners.

Rest assured, you needn't worry that you'll have to memorize a myriad of questions that need answering when you're out shopping; the DNA of my *Style Strategy* consists of three ultra-simple questions anyone can remember. The many answers to these questions—and there are many—will undoubtedly lead you to a style promised land, and save your wallet along the way.

What do I have?

What do I need?

What do I want?

In the following pages, you will learn that when embarking on a shopping extravaganza, the many and multifaceted answers to these three simple questions are far more helpful than a huge bank account. Asking yourself these questions *before* you buy that sleeveless floral-print shift with the adorable ruffles (at such a great price you'd be crazy to pass it up!), or that must-have pleated skirt you saw in the Barneys window on your way to work, will make you so much more of a style maven than you would have been if you spent blindly and shopped without thinking. Shopping smart is pure nirvana when perfectly executed. This book will help show you how to get to this Shopping Shangri-la with a frugal flair that will make you the envy of your former shopaholic self.

Nina

THE Style
tyle
STRATEGY

1

WHAT DO I HAVE?

"In difficult times, fashion is always outrageous."

ELSA SCHIAPARELLI

CHAPTER

ONE

Taking Inventory

THIS IS THE HARD PART. The *really* hard part. For me, anyway. Don't think that I offer the same advice in this section as I've heard others give: "Purge, purge, purge all that's unnecessary, and streamline your closet for a better *you.*" We all know that what we wear isn't the be-all, end-all of our eternal souls. But fashion *is* a key form of self-expression, and just about anything we were once committed to via an actual purchase usually comes with an incredible array of life's great memories. Strategizing what you can and can't live without is hugely important.

I hate the idea of throwing away anything that once thrilled me to euphoric heights. That rush! That feeling most of us get walking out of that amazing boutique, perfect dress, blouse, trousers (whatever!) in hand, our heads held high, our confidence heightened and ready to take on the world. Parting from a garment that saw you through a first date, a job interview, or a fabulous party, a garment that is now entwined with such memories, can be so much harder than you thought. I get it. Ugh—I absolutely get it.

Make no mistake: I don't want you to make a clean sweep and

create an entirely new wardrobe. I simply want you to take stock and rethink your look. My plan is all about having fun while economizing. So rather than going through your clothes and deciding what to get rid of, go through your clothes and decide what you could salvage and repurpose for a new day. By the end of this book, you will have all of the tools necessary to envision your style potential and, even better, achieve it in ways that prevent the needless spending of hard cash. This sorting process is the first step in that direction.

We all have what I call "the old boyfriend pile." The hidden stash of items in the back of your closet that you simply can't bear to part with. You never know when that Norma Kamali sweater dress with the huge shoulder pads, circa 1984, will be in again, right? Actually, it just may be in again now. I know many stylists encourage you to let go of the past when revamping your wardrobe, and it's true that you don't want to appear age inappropriate or as if you're in costume. It can be a fine line between modernizing a vintage ensemble and looking like you haven't gone shopping since college. But if you bring just a few choice pieces back into rotation from time to time, it's not so bad to keep your treasures. Fashion lives in cycles. I have clothes that I was tempted to toss many times and I now bask in the covetous looks I get when I wear them. *And*, I never see anyone else wearing the exact same outfit. Love that!

Like most events that open the doorway for growth in life, taking stock of what you own will make you stronger and better. And it will ultimately fatten up your bank account, too. What's more, the process can be thrilling. Not quite in the same way that Jimmy Choos are, sure. But thrill you, it will. And there's no shame spiral afterward.

So take a deep breath and prepare to go through *everything* in your closet. Everything.

A soundtrack makes everything just a little bit better. I have the perfect playlist for when I clean out my closet. These songs help me rejuvenate my wardrobe and revamp my outlook on life. When I'm ready to put myself into that place where I can begin to challenge my fashion sensibilities and embark on what can be a very emotional closet cleanse, these are some of the songs in my iPod. Making your own playlist is a fun and very useful tool for cracking the whip and setting the mood for achieving your own style goal.

DEPECHE MODE, "CLEAN": Moody, dark, and thumping with a constant beat, this song definitely readies me for letting go of some major closet baggage.

OUTKAST, "SO FRESH, SO CLEAN": The title of this song is the goal of a good closet cleanse, and its catchy chorus sets the tone for the task at hand.

CHRISTINA AGUILERA, "BEAUTIFUL": I love this song. It makes me feel so good about myself and so sad at the same time. The perfect song to listen to when handling those items you loved in their heyday.

MICHAEL JACKSON, "P.Y.T.": The Gloved One in his prime. This song is just fun and it gets me moving. We can all be Pretty Young Things, can't we? Of course.

NO DOUBT, "JUST A GIRL": The California Girl in all of us bursts out in this song. It makes me want to hit the mall, then the beach, then an outdoor concert—all in one day. And then, yes, come home and clean my closet.

BLACK EYED PEAS, "BOOM BOOM POW": I get goosebumps when Fergie sings "Them chickens jackin' my style, I'm so 3008, you so 2000 and late!" So very true, if one maintains their closet they way they should.

BLONDIE, "THE TIDE IS HIGH": Deborah Harry is one of the premiere style icons, and this breezy song hits all the right notes.

MAROON 5, "SHE WILL BE LOVED": The "she" in this song is me. And you. Listen to this and picture yourself in the perfect outfit, in the passenger seat of a perfect convertible.

PRINCE, "RASPBERRY BERET": This song makes me want to wear one. And that alone is reason enough to play it while I make room for new looks.

ABBA, "DANCING QUEEN": Dance while you clean—cardio is good for the soul.

DEEE-LITE, "GROOVE IS IN THE HEART": This song embodies the most fabulous party ever. I just picture the outfit I would wear and I'm inspired for days.

JILL SCOTT, "A LONG WALK": Making room for a new wardrobe can be somewhat like taking a long walk: contemplative, Zen, peaceful, and sometimes just a little wistful.

DESTINY'S CHILD, "SURVIVOR": I am a survivor. And you are as well. This song reminds me that I will get through this process. Nothing better than vintage Destiny's Child to get me where I need to go.

HELEN REDDY, "I AM WOMAN": This song is a classic for a reason. It gets me every time, and makes me unstoppable.

SPICE GIRLS, "SPICE UP YOUR LIFE": So much fun! These gals are so cheeky, and this song inspires me to step everything up a few notches.

MADONNA, "VOGUE": When in doubt, Madonna is the ultimate girl-power, beyond fabulous, style-inspiring music there is. Her songs could make a complete playlist of their own. This is just one of them.

In order to really see what you are working with, you need to take inventory and decide what to do with each item. As you look at each garment, decide whether you want to keep it, get rid of it, alter it, or mend it. This doesn't have to be a chore; it's rather exciting to rediscover things you haven't worn in ten years. Or even two. The trick is to approach it with humor and a damn good sense of fun. Making a party out of a funeral is at the core of this stage in lifting your *Style Strategy* up to the level it should be.

Clean your closet à la *Sex and the City*. You know, the scene in the movie where Carrie Bradshaw is getting ready to move in with Big and tries on all of her clothes for Miranda, Charlotte, and Samantha? Experience your own montage. Invite your girlfriends over to help with the editing. It might even be fun to take pictures for reference and nostalgia. Give yourself at least an afternoon because there *will* be a lot of reminiscing involved (both great and horrendous). Have some cocktails—but not too many; this does require that you be fairly lucid. Then you can return the favor for each of your friends. Make it a rotating, seasonal party. A very close friend of mine, whom I have always admired for her ability to make a good time out of any situation, once told me that giving a "theme" to any gathering instantly makes it a million times better. So, theme it up. Throw a Catwalk Party, for instance, and get set to laugh and cry as you pave the way for renovation.

Go through everything you deem worthy of keeping, piece by piece. Check very carefully for stains and holes. Start thinking about what different things would look good together. If you have a dress made out of a gorgeous silk that you absolutely love, but that just never works with anything else that you own, try to imagine what *would* make it work. Can it be altered? Would it be more versatile as a skirt? Would it be more flattering without pockets? As a sleeveless shift? Belted? Simply reviewing everything you own in its entirety will give you a million ideas for updating your look with what's already in your closet. And, as I said in *The Little Black Book of Style*, your tailor should be one of your best friends.

It is really quite delightful to give your old clothes a new life. By reacquainting yourself with your wardrobe, really studying it, and using your imagination, you will be amazed at how many more outfits you have than you thought. By analyzing garments and picturing how they would look with different pockets, accessories, or trim, you're learning to be your own designer. And you're learning to appreciate good design. You will be personally, not just financially, invested in your clothes. You're training yourself to pay attention to how things

fashion 101

PUT A CORK
UNDER IT

Hard times like wartime or economic downturns often lead to major innovations, especially in fashion. Leather shortages during World War II forced shoe designers to find alternative materials for soles, such as cork and wood. And platforms were instantly all the rage. I can't imagine a world without platforms; what a dull world that would be!

are constructed and what they're made of, which will make you a smarter shopper. And this training carries over into other aspects of your life, too. It's an excellent way to exercise your critical thinking and creativity. Who said fashion is frivolous?

Try things on. Attempt to look at each item in a new way. See if you can identify how pieces could be improved or worn differently. You will develop a better understanding of what looks good on you, what you like, and how you want to present yourself. In other words, you will begin to understand your personal style! And once you understand that, you will project it to the world with a new confidence.

KNOW THYSELF

Now that we're mentally and emotionally prepared, and have a cocktail in hand, we must get to work. Set aside everything that you wear regularly and that is still in good shape, and especially anything that makes you feel fabulous, like your favorite jeans or that vintage pencil skirt. You can build your wardrobe around these basics—your staples. Anything you know accentuates your best physical trait (bust, derrière, waistline, legs, etc.) also accentuates your self-confidence. And you can't put a price tag on that.

Keep an eye out for the timeless, classic pieces. Look for things that you can envision as the foundation of your wardrobe. Clichés usually become clichés because they contain a grain of truth. The simple power of the Little Black Dress or a crisp white shirt is timeless because they go with everything, absolutely everything. They will never go out of style and they're incredibly versatile. More akin to elements such as water and fire, these classic garments were created so that we may live with and appreciate them, forever. If you own one of them, don't throw it away. You'll always regret it.

But the overly trendy we *can* do without. Trends change so often and so drastically in fashion you will want to avoid the extreme ones. To gauge if something is *too* trendy, simply try it on. If you start to feel ridiculous the moment you slip into it or even before that, it's too trendy. Of course, if your friends can't stop laughing when they see you in it or if you suddenly feel the urge to strap on some old school roller skates and rent *Flashdance*, it's definitely time to part with it.

I want to be all that I am capable of becoming.

KATHERINE MANSFIELD

When taking stock of your wardrobe, pay close attention to how the garments are made and what they are made of. If they're made with great fabrics, good tailoring, and are well constructed, they are worth holding on to. Poor construction is never stylish. Wool, cotton, and silk will last forever if you care for them properly—we'll get to that later; it's important—and they seldom look cheap. Some artificial fibers hold up fairly well, but be careful: lower-quality acrylics can get very pilly, especially knits, which can be disastrous when worn past their expiration date.

FABRIC AND CONSTRUCTION

- Wool, cotton, and silk can last a lifetime if you give them love and take good care of them. And they don't look cheap!
- Lower-quality acrylics, especially knits, can get very pilly or become shiny. Not a good look, ladies!
- Hems should always be smooth and flat.
- Seams should be straight and should lie flat as well. Zero puckering is perfection.
- Patterns and stripes should match up at the seams. It looks poorly made when they don't.
- A lining is *always* a good thing. Don't ever let anyone tell you differently. A lining helps create structure and maintains form.

fashion
101

SOMETIMES

LESS IS A

VERY GOOD THING

The scarcity of just about everything during the Civil War led to the decline of the hoop skirt. The hoops were made of metal, a valuable commodity in wartime. Women also needed dresses made with less fabric, and it was necessary that they be able to move easily. Adjusting to these restrictions was the first step on the road to short skirts and trousers. When you think about it, it's pretty marvelous how a style that's born out of lack or a practicality quickly becomes the height of fashion. And thank God we don't have to contend with hoop skirts today!

REVIEW AND REVAMP

Always remember to look at your wardrobe objectively from time to time—at least once a season. It's so easy to fall into the habit of wearing the same blouses with the same skirts, belts, and shoes. Who has time to continually rework their outfits once she's found a combo that makes sense and is remarkably flattering? If you're not made of money, you need to find the time. Even if you *are* made of money, you need to find the time. Doing so can be the difference between unnecessary spending on a dress you'll only wear once, and saving money for the must-have dress you'll get to enjoy for years. In fact, by mixing it up a bit, you may discover that you already own the must-have dress, and what you actually need to buy is the perfect pair of boots to take it from drab to dream.

Holes or thinly worn swaths in a garment can be a blessing in disguise. If a hole sits along a seam it's an easy fix at the tailor. But if the fabric has frayed in a central area, it's rarely possible to mend it invisibly. If the piece is perfect in every other way, pinning on a memorable brooch, sewing on a new pocket, or making some other creative embellishment can cover a multitude of sins. Camouflage the hole and wear it with glee. No one will be the wiser and you may end up wearing quite the conversation piece. Necessity really is the mother of invention.

One thing you can be sure of: There is always a fine line between refurbishing a garment to make it shine again and, pardon the expression, beating a dead horse. Be objective when getting crafty and summoning your inner seamstress (we'll tackle that in Part Three). If it just doesn't seem like it's worth the effort, it probably isn't.

Another thing I almost hate to bring up, but which I am compelled to, is the tragic garment we have all had in our closet: the one we painstakingly wonder if we can save or not. The one we used to love, but which is now diseased with underarm stains. Such items are NOT fixable. Don't think about it at all. Just let it go. Spend your time prolonging the lives of the garments you *can* save. Consider it fashion triage.

Change is the only evidence of life.

EVELYN WAUGH

Taking stock of what you own, when done correctly and thoroughly, actually helps to dampen the urge to shop frivolously. Once you realize how many different options are already in your closet, you'll be able to channel your shopping energy more productively. So when that urge strikes, don't give in. Put on some makeup, do your hair, and then try on your own clothes in front of the mirror. Combine garments in a completely new way. Play dress-up. Don't think about where you'll wear these outfits. Just have fun with it. Believe me, you will discover that your wardrobe is much more versatile than you thought, and it will *feel* like shopping.

But without the guilt.

" Walk to the edge. Listen hard. Play with abandon. Laugh. Choose with no regret. Continue to learn. Do what you love. Live as if this is all there is. "

MARY ANNE RADMACHER

CHAPTER

TWO

Saving the Basics
and Saying Good-bye

YOUR CLOSET IS CLEAN. NOW WHAT?

Every wardrobe needs a solid foundation. The glitter comes later.
So, follow me.

You must figure out what's missing from your closet. To know
what you need, you've got to know what the basics are. Luckily, my
two previous books, *The Little Black Book of Style* and *The One Hun-
dred*, contain everything there is to know about the essentials every
fabulously stylish woman must own. I put a lot of work into making
the lists in those books and I will always swear by them.

But, just in case you haven't read them, here's the short list of classic must-haves:

- Classic high-heeled pump
- Ballet flats
- Trench coat
- Classic white shirt
- The Little Black Dress or LBD
- Cashmere cardigan or turtleneck
- A great bag
- Denim

Own them, have them, love them. This is your foundation; your look is built upon this list.

Design is a constant challenge
to balance comfort with luxe,
the practical with the desirable.

DONNA KARAN

Because we're being frugal *and* creative, I'm encouraging you to revamp rather than discard. But this is not always possible. Sometimes you have to let things go. And breaking up with your ex-favorite pair of jeans, or dress, or turtleneck can be a painful experience. So here are some tips.

Don't bother saving anything that just doesn't fit you anymore. Ill-fitting clothes are absolutely deadly to your self-esteem. There's no reason to let that gorgeous skirt—it was a steal, but you can't zip it up, and truth be told, it was always a little too tight—taunt you from your closet. Nothing makes you feel thinner than wearing clothes that truly fit properly.

Be merciless if you have limited storage. Many of us have lived in those tiny apartments, with makeshift closets (storage bins under the bed, for instance). Pack-ratting clothes that you never wear anyway can make your living space a living nightmare, and this state of chaos ultimately does affect what you choose to wear. If you don't have the space, get rid of anything that's too trendy or too last season, or that you haven't worn in the past year.

Always keep in mind, this doesn't mean throwing these items away. *Reduce. Reuse. Recycle.* These three *R*s will not only save the planet, but your closet as well. Find a charity to which you can donate anything that is still wearable. One woman's trash is another's treasure, and it's tax-deductible. Be sure to research the charity before you donate. Verify that it's legitimate and that, if they are reselling the clothes, a significant amount of the proceeds will indeed go to the needy. If you have things that are just so tattered that there's no help for them, use them as cleaning cloths or find out where you can recycle textiles in your community. Believe it or not, it's possible to make paper out of recycled cotton, linen, and silk. It's the environmentally healthy option, and in today's well-informed world, we should all know better.

All that is not eternal is eternally out of date.

C. S. LEWIS

Again, check everything very carefully for holes, stains, and other signs of wear-and-tear such as thin spots or fading. It won't matter if it's Chanel or Balenciaga; a glaring flaw is the only thing anyone will notice. If you can't bear to part with a damaged garment, put it in your "fix it" pile and start thinking about ways to mask or repair the problem. Don't hesitate to consult with your tailor about ways to revive the dead. But if it's really gone, hold a candlelight vigil and move on.

You've taken the first step toward discovering the hidden potential in what you already own by understanding the elements involved with answering the **What Do I Have?** stage of your *Style Strategy*. Your look is beginning to take root. Your closet should look fresh, and you should feel inspired by what you just accomplished (if not slightly drunk from the Champagne you and your friends sipped while getting to work).

So let's now go over how to further bid farewell to the hurdles that keep you from unleashing the style diva within—in a more detailed, productive, and eco-friendly way—by moving on to understanding the potential of the answers to the second question in your *Style Strategy:* **What Do I Need?**

2

WHAT DO I NEED?

"Bling is over. Red-carpetry-covered-with-rhinestones is out. I call it 'the new modesty.'"

KARL LAGERFELD

CHAPTER

THREE

The Fashion Foundation

THE POSITIVITY that so many of my friends and die-hard fashionistas have been expressing in the face of economic difficulty is truly inspiring. Optimism may not save the world, but a heavy dose of it can't hurt. So many people I've talked to lately have gushed about how happy they are that the pressure to maintain the trappings of affluence is lifting. About how refreshing it is that people are getting back to basics. And these are people who were once absolutely obsessed with labels—the more expensive, the better. Now, when you'd expect just the opposite, they are utterly aglow with a new sense of freedom. They don't have to buy the very latest thing. Instead they are reveling in the newfound joy of rediscovering the simple pleasures in life: reconnecting with family and friends, evenings in, a renewed sense of community, and a sense of responsibility to that community. Suddenly a Prius is a greater status symbol than an Escalade. I think we can all take heart in the knowledge that reevaluating one's priorities is the rule of the day. Ostentatious displays of wealth are out. Sophisticated, eco-friendly, panache is in.

Following my *Style Strategy* is like putting your shopping habits on a diet. Count your financial calories every day, and before you know it, you can have that occasional piece of cake—guilt-free! And you'll look fantastic. When you're tempted to fall off the wagon and splurge, remember that you'll just have to tighten your belt (the one that's already in your closet) later in the month. It's not about deprivation; it's about prioritization. Sensibility and smart shopping are the new black. Remember the mantra: **Shop smart, stay chic, and make it last.**

If I can have any impact, I want women to feel good about themselves and have fun with fashion.

MICHELLE OBAMA

JUST THE BASICS

In this section, we're focusing strictly on the basics of your wardrobe. The must-haves. But don't worry, the cake and shimmer will come later. After all, frivolity is just as essential as the basics. I, for one, don't want you to think I've lost my love for the fun layered into the shopping experience. But in today's world, it's all about balance.

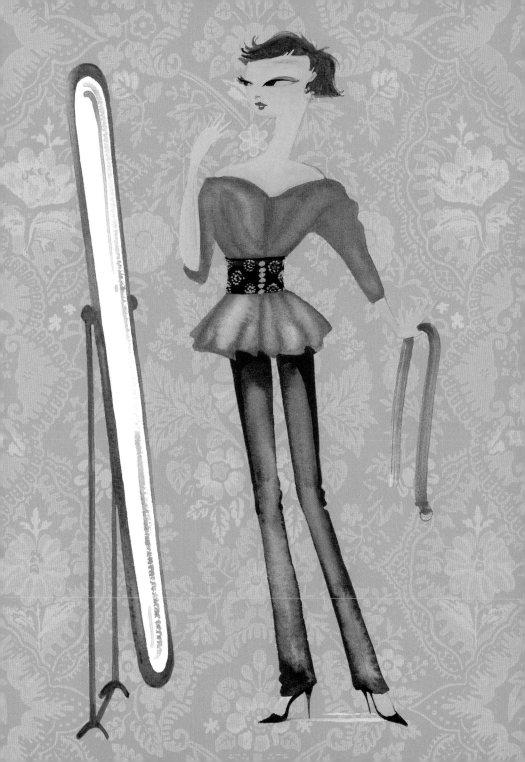

We've all seen, and envied, that woman who walks into the room with an air of effortless chic. Everything about her just *works*. She exudes confidence, and you know she doesn't spend hours trying on outfit after outfit, exchanging accessories, worrying about whether her shoes look good with her skirt. Well, she probably *does* worry about all of those things (since everyone does from time to time), but her confidence comes from enjoying the *process*, and from knowing that she's got the essentials covered. She knows her anchor pieces are strong, so she can have some fun with colorful trimmings or statement pieces. Pretty soon, that woman we all aspire to emulate will be you.

So, here we are. Phase Two. You've reacquainted yourself with your closet; you've paid a visit to the tailor and worked with him to find ways of making your visions a reality. Even more satisfying, perhaps you've planned some projects for yourself. You've recapped the basics, and you've donated or given a proper burial to the garments you just couldn't save. Now you can round out this part of your style transformation by filling in the gaps. You are building a solid foundation for your overall look, and this foundation must be sound, sturdy, and spectacular.

The genius of this *Style Strategy* is that as you remodel your wardrobe and build this foundation, you can get more and more creative with each step, so by the time you've finished the book and unleashed your inner diva, not only will you look smashing, but you'll be newly empowered with the confidence that you *own* your look.

MAKE A LIST

First things first, though. Make a list of what has survived your recent closet purge. A *written* list. I know it sounds tedious, but mark my words, in addition to pinpointing the blanks in your wardrobe, it will prevent the shame spiral brought on by impetuous purchases. If you're anything like me, no matter how many clothes you have, it always seems as though your closet is full of *nothing to wear.* You know how it goes—water, water everywhere, but not a drop to drink. I'm constantly rummaging through my closet in my head, planning outfits for upcoming events. The options are endless. It's my job, after all! But when it's time for me to get dressed, there are days when my ideas go right out the window. My fashion ADD gets even worse when I go shopping. I love clothes! I want everything! And this is exactly where the list comes in. It's all about priorities and keeping your fashion focus in check.

Second, of course, you have to make another list of what you *need.* Not *want,* but *need.* Write down the basics missing from your closet. This will be your reference for shopping. Keep it in your wallet and refer to it frequently, especially before you actually lay down any cash.

And last but not least, it's essential that you know which of these basics you might have to save up for. There are numerous pieces that you can get away with faking a bit, but the real load-bearing wall of your fashion foundation requires an investment. And you should think of it that way: long-term. These are pieces that you will love and cherish and pass down to your children. *If* you follow my advice.

CAN BUY ME LOVE

It's true. In my opinion, the Beatles may have gotten it wrong on this one. But it depends on what we mean by *love*. In today's world, we're all so busy. There are never enough hours in the day to accomplish everything you need to do, much less spend quality time with those you so deeply want to. A simple shopping excursion to the mall can be a real bonding experience. What better way to enjoy the company of those you love (girlfriends, mother, daughter, niece, etc.) than passing a leisurely afternoon browsing at the mall together? The experience can be bliss for all involved.

You don't actually have to spend a lot of money. Revel in the moment. Ask your shopping partner what he or she loves and why. Point out what you love and why. Find things that you think would look good on her. One of my fondest teenage memories is of my best friend and me taking her little brother shopping for "cool" clothes when he turned fourteen. It was so fun to help him learn to develop his personal style. He was our life-size dress-up doll, and we were so proud to have a hand in his blossoming into the cute boy in school. My best friend and I will forever cherish the memory of that shopping trip. Do the same with your BFF.

Always keep in mind that shopping-as-bonding is not *only* about the purchase. It's about sharing ideas, learning each other's taste, and getting inspiration for outfits of your own. And of course, who doesn't secretly think she can make her friends, sister, or mom look and feel better about themselves with a little fashion advice from an expert? After reading this book, you are this expert.

A LITTLE INSPIRATION

- Pick out an ensemble for each other to try on. It's so illuminating to see how you look in clothes that you wouldn't normally choose for yourself.
- Be each other's mirror. Encourage and uplift one another. Take the opportunity to pay your loved one some compliments, and point out what makes her look gorgeous.
- Split up and give yourselves half an hour to buy each other a present for under $10, something that you know your friend would never buy for herself. You'd be surprised how quickly your style boundaries will change upon learning what your friends think you are capable of.
- Talk each other down when you're tempted to splurge on something unnecessary.
- Take a breather: people-watch and gossip over coffee. Relaxing is part of the shopping experience—one must never forget this essential part of your shopping foray.

"We are shaped and fashioned by what we love."

JOHANN WOLFGANG VON GOETHE

CHAPTER

FOUR

Making Investments

SOMETIMES you just have to drop a little cash. It's inevitable. Replacing buttons on an old frock only goes so far. The basics are your wardrobe's building blocks, the structure upon which your look is crafted, so they need to last. It doesn't do you any good to live in a solid gold castle if it's built on Styrofoam blocks.

When you're on a budget, it can be a little daunting to spend $300 on a pair of boots or a coat. But just remember that these items should last for *years*, not a single season. I will give you the keys to understanding and recognizing quality materials and craftsmanship. Once you know what to look for, you will appreciate what makes a quality garment, not just the designer label, and you will be able to invest with confidence. It really does pay to be an educated consumer. Just keep these two concepts in mind: *quality* and *classic*. Your basics should be understated; let your individuality shine through your accent pieces and accessories.

It's absolutely essential to know the difference between "inexpensive" and "cheap," *and* what makes a bargain. So here's a little reminder.

Cheap: Even expensive clothing can look cheap. It's the characteristics of the garment rather than the cost that defines the quality of clothing. A cheap garment makes people wonder how little you spent on it. Ask yourself:

- Is it poorly made? (I'll go into specifics later.)
- Could this micromini be a little too risqué? Hooker chic is never a good thing.
- Does this material *look* too synthetic? Synthetics are wonderful, but if you glance at the fabric and think that you will have to avoid open flames while wearing it, it most definitely looks too synthetic.

Inexpensive: This means well-made but low-cost clothing in wearable fabrics. Inexpensive garments don't make people think about how much you spent on them, they just wonder where they can get one, too. Inexpensive is a good thing.

Bargain: Well-made, *expensive* clothing that, with my guidance and your great eye and shopping savvy, you find at a fantastic discount. A bargain makes you want to announce the price every time someone asks you where you got it. Don't. But you'll want to! A great bargain is the smart-shopping nirvana we already touched upon, which we will feel if we go about things the right way.

It goes without saying: Always avoid anything that *looks* cheap. Knowing when you *can't* fake it is just as important as knowing *how* to fake it. Another very important, and related, distinction is the (very fine) line between cheesy or tacky and kitschy. We must understand the difference between these three if we're going to successfully morph our *Style Strategy* into something that yields results.

THERE IS A FINE LINE

KITSCHY: A GOOD THING

- Betty Draper on *Mad Men*
- A vintage, white, faux Christmas tree
- Dita Von Teese
- Wearing a Chanel suit accessorized with '80s jewelry
- A bark cloth, Hawaiian-print maxi dress

CHEESY OR TACKY: A BAD THING

- Peg and Kelly Bundy on *Married with Children*
- Chenille patterned sweaters or Christmas sweaters with snowmen or other holiday motifs
- Making yourself over to look like a carbon copy of Bettie Page
- Wearing head-to-toe emblems or labels
- A rayon Hawaiian shirt

If you aren't confident that you know the difference between cheesy, tacky, and kitschy, don't risk going there.

If I had to choose just one thing—in my wardrobe, let's not get crazy!—to spend money on, it would be shoes. It's the golden rule that most fashionistas know, but it bears repeating here. Over and over. When I was a little girl, I loved, absolutely *loved*, to dress up in a green chiffon party dress with a rhinestone collar and a pair of silver heels that belonged to my grandmother when she was young. Those silver shoes made me feel like a princess. I would probably wear them today if they still existed. A great shoe can make a $20 outfit look like couture, and a poorly constructed shoe can make couture look like a cheap knockoff. OK, that may be a slight exaggeration, but we've all heard the expression "the clothes make the man." Well, it *should* be "the *shoes* make the man"—or woman. When you meet someone, don't you check out their footwear immediately? For me, it's almost a reflex. Your footwear has the unique ability to make your legs look longer and more shapely, to balance your proportions, and add that certain *je ne sais quoi* to an ensemble. Shoes can dress an outfit up or make it seem casual. They project an attitude. They make you feel sexy. In literature and film, they're often imbued with magical powers. *There's no place like home . . .* That said, I'm going to give you a *lot* of advice about shoes.

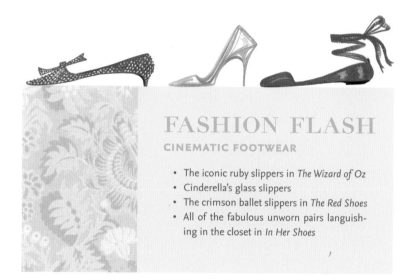

FASHION FLASH
CINEMATIC FOOTWEAR

- The iconic ruby slippers in *The Wizard of Oz*
- Cinderella's glass slippers
- The crimson ballet slippers in *The Red Shoes*
- All of the fabulous unworn pairs languishing in the closet in *In Her Shoes*

This doesn't mean you need to invest in an array of $600 Manolo Blahniks and Jimmy Choos—although a girl can dream! You just have to know what to look for, what looks good on you, and to be prepared to spend a little cash. You're making a long-term investment, so it pays to err on the conservative side when you're selecting a style. You don't have to be boring, just avoid anything too extreme or too trendy. Your motto should always be "keep it simple."

SIZE MATTERS

Have your feet professionally measured so that you know your correct shoe size. Properly fitting shoes look better, feel better, and last longer. Don't go by what size you were when you were sixteen. Bodies change, age creeps in, and yes, our feet expand. A terrible reality, but one we must face when investing in the perfect shoe. The stakes are way too high.

How can you tell if a shoe is worth the investment? What exactly should you look for when choosing a style? It's simple.

- TOE: When you are shopping for a classic shoe or boot, avoid extremes—really pointy, really square, really round. Overly square toes are a pet peeve of mine as they can make feet and toes look too wide and clumsy. Shoe styles change constantly, and the toe is the first thing you see. Remember, we're working on the basics, and they should be timeless. (I know I'm being repetitive, but it's for your own good! Remember this whenever you're tempted to go to extremes.) The ideal toe is slightly tapered and beautifully shaped, with rounded edges. Pay attention to the details. Subtle accents like seams, stitching, or piping can really make a simple shoe stand out—in a good way or a bad one. Be careful. Know the difference.

· HEEL: Overly thick square heels are another pet peeve of mine. Especially when they're attached to slides, sandals, and flip-flops. This style is so tragically clunky and unflattering; unless you have unusually long, thin legs, they can actually make you look a tad stocky. The goal is always to elongate your silhouette whenever possible— right, ladies?

A gracefully curved and slightly tapered heel looks good on everyone, no matter what type of shoe—pump, flat, wedge. Avoid anything that flares out toward the bottom, á la Lady Miss Kier from Deee-Lite, circa 1990. Again, details, details, details! Pay attention to the color of the edges of the sole and the heel; it should complement the rest of the shoe. Think of Christian Louboutin's signature red sole. So subtle. So unique. So pure. So beautiful!

· MATERIALS: Smooth leather is the most practical choice. Provided the leather is real and not fake, it will age better and have a nicer patina. Patent leather doesn't go with everything and suede is hard to care for. Also, avoid golds or silvers that are too shiny, as such shocking hues mostly scream cheap. You'll get the most out of your dollar if your investment shoe is as simple as possible.

- CONSTRUCTION: How a shoe is put together is just as important as its style. Perhaps even more important. A well-crafted shoe will last for years. It's worth the investment. And, although it may require some time to break in, it will be infinitely more comfortable than a poorly made shoe. Once you've worn them a few times, good leather shoes will mold to your foot without losing their shape—if they are the correct size. Check the seams and the stitching carefully. Especially when you're buying boots—they have more of everything. The seams should be straight and flat, creating a beautifully streamlined effect. If they are crooked, bunchy, puckered, or the thread ends are showing, they will fall apart more quickly, and they just won't look good. When boot shopping, also pay particular attention to the zipper and how the shaft is connected to the foot (it should be shapely). The zipper should be subtle (unless its visibility is part of the design) and the slider should glide smoothly. Glue is frequently used with man-made materials like rubber or pleather, which is fine, as long as it doesn't show. But keep an eye out for globs around the edges of the sole—a very bad look. It's always preferable for the sole to be sewn on, a sign of a truly well-made shoe. I'm sure this goes without saying, but molded, faux stitching, faux wood grain, or other texture on a plastic sole is definitely a no-no.

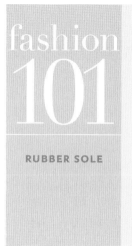

fashion
101

RUBBER SOLE

Repurposed materials were just about the only ones available during the Great Depression. Back then people used old seat covers from cars to make clothes for everyday wear, and the Red Cross held a shoe drive where they collected worn-out shoes, took them apart, and reassembled them using old tires as soles.

Today, Melissa Shoes has an incredible patented material called MELFLEX, a hypoallergenic rubber that is flexible, durable, recycled, *and* recyclable. Betsey Johnson recently designed a limited-edition line for them. I love them; they're made in Brazil and they're green.

When women say, "How high should my heel be?"
I say, "How high can you handle and
stay in for two hours without having two Advil?"

MICHAEL KORS

If you see a pair of shoes that make you gasp, and your heart beats a little faster, try them on—and then immediately leave the store. If they aren't on your **What Do I Need?** list, don't buy them. Even if you're madly in love. Before you do anything rash, take a deep breath and run home to read Part Three of this book. At the very least, wait a day or two and if you're still dreaming about them, see if you can find

them at a lower price online. If that doesn't cure you, then it's time to start saving. And go buy that shoe when you can afford to pay cash. Putting in that little extra effort will make you love them even more. And when you love what you're wearing, it shows.

SHOES: THE ABOVE AND BEYOND LIST

These go a bit beyond the basics, so once you've got the bare minimum covered, this list will help you enhance your collection. Have I mentioned that I love shoes?

Knee-High, High-Heeled Boots: So sexy! You can wear them with anything: skirts, jeans, trousers, you name it. They instantly add a little spice to any outfit. As soon as I zip up a pair of beautifully made high-heeled boots, I've lost ten pounds, I'm ten years younger, and I feel amazing.

I'm told leather drives men up the wall.
I like wearing it because it feels nice.

HONOR BLACKMAN

A rich chocolate- or coffee-colored leather boot is luxurious and classic. Black is always fabulous and edgy, and if you can't live without a black boot (many women can't), go for it. But do consider the versatility of brown. Yes, black does match everything, but a really deep, beautiful brown complements most colors without being harsh. And, as long as you keep them in excellent condition, brown boots dress up spectacularly well.

THE PERFECT FIT

Boots that you plan to wear with skirts or under trousers should fit your calves snugly, with no more than a ¼" gap at the top. The ankle should have enough room for movement. Remember, when they're new, boots are slightly taller, so keep in mind that they will sit a little farther below your knee once the ankle has worn in. Obviously you need a roomier fit if you plan to tuck your pants into them. Slouchier styles can be very fashion forward, but unless you are tall and slim, they may not be particularly flattering, so keep this in mind.

Riding Boots: These days we have an extravagant variety of height, color, and embellishment to choose from when picking boots. Riding boots are definitely a classic, and although not a must-have for every day, they are certainly versatile. They're casual-chic, can be worn with skirts or trousers, and they're comfortable to walk in. Look for a streamlined boot, not too chunky at the toe and heel. Do not confuse this style with motorcycle boots! Motorcycle boots are also great, but they're a tad too edgy for most, and not quite as versatile as riding boots.

CUSTOMIZE

If you have a hard time finding boots to fit your legs, look online for custom-fitted calf-high boots. There are several companies in the UK that will ship to the United States. They're quite reasonably priced and come in a great variety of styles. Even if you don't have trouble with fit, what is more luxurious than custom-made boots?

Classic High-Heel Pumps: So many options, I don't even know where to begin! I love mary janes with a delicate ankle strap, but I also love a simple, beautifully crafted basic pump. You know best what style flatters your legs. Try on lots of pairs and find one that's comfortable and sophisticated, in a neutral tone like black, brown, gray, or bone. Look for exquisitely subtle details such as piping or texture. And it goes without saying—but I will say it again—you want these shoes to last, so avoid very square, very round, or very pointy toes. They will end up looking dated.

Ballet Flats: Every chic woman *must* have an adorable pair of ballet flats. They're beyond timeless and essential; they embody the gamine spirit. I think everyone agrees that Audrey Hepburn wore them best—in just about every one of her movies. If I'm not picturing her wearing the iconic Little Black Dress in *Breakfast at Tiffany's*, I imagine her in a black turtleneck, black cigarette pants, and black ballet flats. So effortlessly chic! As a schoolgirl, I remember absolutely *yearning* for a pair of black Mia flats. I wore them until the soles were paper thin. And then I bought a new pair. They're that delicious.

THESE SHOES WERE MADE FOR WALKING

Of course you want to look fabulous, but you need shoes you can wear all day without severe pain. Nothing makes me crankier than uncomfortable shoes, and crankiness is highly contagious in the office. So it's in your best interest to know how to find a comfortable pair. For everyone's sake.

- Always buy the correct size! *ALWAYS!*
- Leather molds to your foot, which is a good thing. But keep in mind that leather shoes will stretch a little.
- Don't try on shoes first thing in the morning, or after you've been on your feet all day. Trust me, you'll regret it.

We all need a splash of bad taste.
No taste is what I am against.

DIANA VREELAND

Stilettos: A *must* for cocktail parties—actually, a must for *any* party. Open- or closed-toe, whichever you prefer. It's worth spending a little extra on these; cheap stilettos *look* cheap and they're guaranteed to be uncomfortable. Take some time picking these out. They're for special occasions and party frocks. They have to be glamorous and sexy, but they also have to be versatile. Just as important, you want to able to wear them for at least a couple of hours without crying from the pain. And believe it or not, a well-made stiletto *can* be comfortable (relatively speaking). The fit of the toe (not too tight), the width of the heel (not too narrow), and placement of the arch (your foot should be fully supported by the sole, with no gaps at the arch) are key. A slight platform looks fabulous with spike heels, but don't go higher than ¾ of an inch—remember, timeless is what we're striving for. And you don't want to break your neck. Nothing ruins a party faster than a trip to the emergency room.

Instant gratification is not soon enough.

MERYL STREEP

EXCEPTIONS TO THE RULE

There are always exceptions. Here are some shoes that *don't* have to be an investment.

Sandals: There is a plethora of inexpensive, cute, and fun sandals in this world. You don't need to spend a fortune on these; after all, you're wearing them to the beach, on picnics, just about everywhere in the summer. Go crazy with color; sandals are supposed to be casual and flirty.

Espadrilles: Espadrilles are a phenomenal spring/summer option. If a shoe evokes the heroine of a Hemingway novel, it's guaranteed to be stylish and fresh. Low heels, platforms, solids, stripes—go for it. Be prepared for comments galore when you own a good pair of these Spanish classics.

Sneakers: I'm an advocate of both exercise and comfort, and sneakers fit the bill. Converse, Keds, Sauçony, Nike, Adidas, Puma—the possibilities are endless. But remember where to wear them and where not to wear them. The gym, yoga, hiking, OK. Everywhere else, not OK.

Caress the detail, the divine detail.

VLADIMIR NABOKOV

THE WORLD BEYOND SHOES

Yes, there is one. And here is your introduction to it. The more information on the basics you can get your hands on, the more options you'll have to play with when accentuating those basics. The following is my take on the basics I think you should make priorities. But by no means are these the *only* items that are considered basics. Point of view is everything in fashion, which is why your personal spin on any basic can become the spine of your style body.

Put on a trench, you're suddenly Audrey Hepburn
walking along the Seine, even if
you've got red hair and you're five-one.

MICHAEL KORS

Trench Coat: A perennial classic, a great trench coat is universally flattering and practical. It has been the outerwear of choice for cinema's best spies, femmes fatales, and moguls. You have so many different versions of the classic trench to choose from that it can be a bit overwhelming. If you live in a cold climate, consider a wool coat; in a medium climate, cotton with a removable lining. The perfect trench looks equally good buttoned, belted, or open. The length is completely up to you—I find that just below the knee is the most versatile.

Classic White Shirt: This is a staple. A perfectly tailored white shirt evokes an air of cool, soigné sophistication. It's up to you whether to go for a more fitted version or a crisp, slightly oversized style. A fitted shirt should skim your body, with no gapping at the bust or pulling across the shoulders, and you should be able to move your arms comfortably. Uma Thurman wore it iconically in *Pulp Fiction*.

Soft cotton pants should be avoided
if one is going anywhere other than the yoga studio.

TIM GUNN

Trousers: A good pair of light wool trousers can be worn almost any time of year. Sailor pants with wide legs are almost universally flattering and elegant. As long as you feel comfortable and confident in them, just about any style will work. Again, choose a solid, neutral color; a simple cut; and avoid extremes like flares or very tapered legs. And no front pleats unless you are unusually skinny! Choose a dark gray or brown, perhaps with a subtle pinstripe, although solids are the best for versatility.

fashion
101

CUFF SUPPRESSANT

During WWII, when everything was in short supply, cuffs were considered a waste of fabric, so they fell out of fashion. This is yet another example of how many trends are born from necessity.

Skirt: A-line or pencil, or one of each (at a minimum). With a hemline just above or just below the knee. You know what looks best on you and what makes you feel stunning. Wool for fall and winter; cotton for spring and summer. Every woman needs at least one black skirt. Go for dark solids or subtle prints in muted colors. Pencil skirts are chic and have just a touch of sexiness. A-lines are flattering to almost every body type; they're easy and comfortably sophisticated. A bit of embellishment like a front pocket or piping is always nice; just avoid appliqués or very loud trimming. Remember, versatility equals longevity.

IN THE KNOW

NO ONE PUTS A SMART SHOPPER IN A CORNER!

A good rule to follow: Don't buy anything unless you have at least three items in your closet that it will go with. The smart woman always creates options. She is never, ever cornered.

Blazer: A fabulous tailored blazer or jacket over just about any ensemble creates a casual-chic and put-together look. There are so many options and I love them all: denim, leather, wool, cotton, corduroy, jean jacket, suit jacket, tweed, boxy, three-quarter sleeve—I could go on and on. Since we're focusing on basics here, I advise you to have at least one suit-style jacket—fitted or boxy, whichever you prefer. I like fitted myself.

Buying is a profound pleasure.

SIMONE DE BEAUVOIR

Little Black Dress: Of course, no list of basics is complete without the ubiquitous LBD. A simple black shift can be accessorized in so many different ways; it's really like having a closet full of dresses. You just have to use your imagination and choose the perfect frock. Pick a matte fabric that's not too stretchy. Wool crepe is a perfect option. As always, fit is important. The ideal dress should hug your curves without pulling anywhere. If necessary, have it tailored—it's so worth it. A sure way to end up on the worst-dressed list is by wearing an ill-fitting gown. Remember the loose bodice on Gwyneth Paltrow's pink Ralph Lauren at the 1999 Oscars? She was a gorgeous woman (who won an Oscar in 2004, no less) in a gorgeous dress and the fashion police focused on her gappy bustline.

Once you have the perfect dress, you can add a belt, a brooch, a scarf, a long necklace, different stockings, different shoes—the possibilities are endless. Use accessories to lend individuality, a touch of color, and flair to your frock. Angelina Jolie wore a simple, strapless black Elie Saab dress to the 2009 Oscars with a beautiful, deep-green emerald ring and matching earrings. Her jewelry added just a touch of vivid color, transforming her look from understated to uniquely striking.

A SUBTLE HINT OF LADY

Wear a slip with lacy trim or a ruffle that is just a tiny bit longer than your dress. There is even a clothing line called Your Slip is Showing that offers slips trimmed with ostrich feathers, rhinestones, velvet, etc., designed specifically for this purpose. *Uber chic.*

A Great Bag: All a girl needs is a sturdy, roomy, yet classically stylish leather bag for every day and a sparkly, adorable clutch, just big enough for ID, money, and lipstick for evening. Anything more is gravy.

I used to buy good shoes; now I buy good bags.
They make me feel more confident.

MARC JACOBS

Cardigan or Turtleneck Sweater: Both are great for layering. Cashmere is so warm and lightweight and *soft!* You must have at least one. Borrow your boyfriend's sweater. In the '90s, Kurt Cobain single-handedly reinstituted the cardigan as a staple for men. Throw a cardigan over a lacy camisole or LBD and you're all set to go from office to evening. The Gap all but reinvented the cardigan, with a line of twenty-two colors and a series of custom versions created by twenty students from the Rhode Island School of Design. Go team!

fashion
101

**TAKING IT TO
THE STREETS**

Because cars were scarce during WWI, women started bicycling everywhere instead, and that's when cross-body, messenger-style bags became popular. They were actually considered avant-garde then; now, we'd be lost without them. Especially in a bustling city.

All the ladies in the house let me hear you scream
"We love the way we look in our jeans"

GRANDMASTER FLASH, "THEM JEANS," 1987

Denim: It's imperative that you own a great-fitting pair of jeans; nothing's better for your self-esteem. And expensive doesn't always equal a great fit. It's best to have one or two pairs of dark-rinse jeans (very slimming) and boot-cut jeans (flattering on just about every body type) in your arsenal. These jeans should sit just below the waist (not too low-rise, but definitely not Mom jeans either). They're dressy-casual, sexy without trying too hard, and you can always throw them on when you don't know what to wear. Try on a ton of styles in different price ranges; there's so much variety, you're guaranteed to find the perfect pair eventually. Once you've found the cut that's most flattering on you and you know the correct size, look online for bargains. Old Navy, Target, Gap, and JCPenney have a great variety of fits and styles, as do higher-end brands like 7 For All Mankind, Lucky Brand, Earl, and True Religion. Everyone should be able to find something on-trend that makes her derrière look the way she wants it to.

Don't spend a lot of money on extreme styles like super-skinny jeans, bling-encrusted, and huge bell-bottoms (in fact, you probably want to avoid bling-encrusted and huge bell-bottoms in general). If you're struggling—I know jean shopping can be traumatic—try a custom-fit boutique. There are quite a few online options. They take your measurements, you choose the rinse, cut, stretch, pockets, details, etc., and you get a great pair of jeans without leaving the house!

I always check in the mirror
to make sure nothing is see-through.

SCARLETT JOHANSSON

Lingerie: This falls somewhere between the basics and the cheap thrills (they're coming). We all wear underwear. And I think it's safe to say that we all have very specific and personal preferences in that area. I only have two rules. Number one, make sure it fits properly! Go to a lingerie store and find out what your true bra size is. So many women don't wear the correct bra and it can make an enormous difference in the way your clothes look. Number two, own at least a few pieces of sexy lingerie. Wear it when you need a little extra confidence, even if you're the only one who knows.

So now you have the basics, and a little extra. Splurge on at least two pair of everyday shoes or boots. Splurge on a good trench coat, an LBD, one or two skirts, a jacket, a tailored shirt, and a pair of trousers. Everything else is filler. Gloriously beautiful filler, but certainly not absolute essentials.

With the building blocks in place, you are free to indulge when you can afford to—just keep your list handy! Recite the mantra. And read on.

fashion
101

Parachute silk was used to make undergarments during WWII. Even in wartime, women understood the importance of silk lingerie.

GERONIMO!

People ask how I can play with all those rings,
and I reply, "Very well, thank you."

LIBERACE

IN THE KNOW

BUY-POLAR SHOPPING

For every glittering, glamorous, luxury shopping destination, there's an equally glittering, glamorous, less expensive counterpart. Take a tour of the global fashion capitals throughout the world and experience the yin and yang of the shopping experience. These are some of my must-go shopping stops when traveling. Don't miss visiting each, as you never know what you may find. The perfect mix of high and low in any ensemble is the key to having that great look we all strive for.

	HIGH	LOW
NEW YORK	Barneys	Macy's
LONDON	Harrods	Debenhams
MADRID	Salamanca	El Corte Inglés
PARIS	Galeries Lafayette	Monoprix
TOKYO	Takashimaya	Tobu/Metropolitan Plaza

GRADUATING INTO
YOUR DAZZLE

Some pieces don't need to last forever. Phew!
With these, you can have more fun, mix it up a
bit, and be a little impractical. Just because you
don't want to spend a fortune on trends doesn't
mean you can't look *au courant*. Once you've established a base of timeless and classic pieces,
you can add a few inexpensive, frou-frou touches
without looking like a fashion victim.

   Having conquered the basics, the sky really
is the limit. The world is your oyster. Everything
else is cake. And I did say that we'd get to that. So,
just by following my lead up to this point, you're
done, you're dressed, you're stylish, you're
fabulous. You've got what you need. But don't
you always want more? Of course you do! Every
woman wants to pamper herself, and I firmly
believe that feeling pampered and indulged is
a vital part of projecting style. If you don't indulge yourself occasionally, you go through life
with the nagging feeling that something's missing, that you're not quite fulfilled. It's the same
reason why most diets fail. And this emptiness
will inevitably impair your ability to sashay into
a room projecting an air of serene confidence
and self-possession.

In August, in the Italian squares flooded
by dazzling light and torrid silence,
the black or gray hat of the passerby
floats along sadly, like dung.
"Color! We need color to compete
with the Italian Sun!"

FROM THE FUTURIST MANIFESTO OF
THE ITALIAN HAT, 1933,
MARINETTI, PRAMPOLINI, SOMENZI

The last step of my Strategy will help you answer the question: *What Do I Want?* Yes, it's easy to think of a million things that you want. But when you're on a budget, you have to come up with a realistic list that actually does make you feel fabulous. It is possible, and really quite simple; you just need to prioritize and be imaginative. And when you discover that your own creativity allows you to attain these luxuries, you will appreciate them all the more.

So read on!

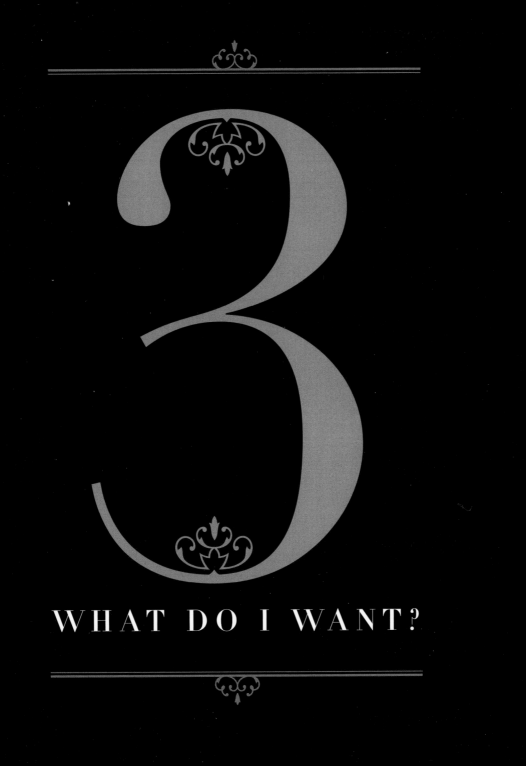

3

WHAT DO I WANT?

BLANCHE: Well, Dorothy, since when do you care about what you look like?

DOROTHY: Ever since I came down from the bell-tower and had my hump fixed."

FROM *THE GOLDEN GIRLS*

CHAPTER

FIVE

Pampering Yourself

O F THE THREE CORE QUESTIONS that constitute the DNA of a solid *Style Strategy*, **What Do I Want?** is the easiest to answer. I think it's safe to say that we all know what we want. I could fill a book with what I want. In fact, I have. So the trick here is to get what you want without spending what you don't have. And it's not as hard as it may seem. You just have to think uniquely, and be a little playful.

Some days I wake up with an irresistible desire to go shopping. I just want *something*. It almost doesn't even matter what it is. I have a persistent yearning that seems as though it can only be quelled with the purchase of a cute pair of shoes or a fabulous cocktail dress. Such desperate yearning overcomes all of us on occasion. And retail therapy is the easy fix. It meets our need to feel fresh and pretty and glamorous, in an instant. It fills our desire to go to our "happy place" where everything is clean and crisp and *new*. The belief held by most nutritionists—that if you deprive yourself, you'll fall off the wagon and binge—holds true for shopping, too (proving again, that a style budget really is quite similar to a diet). We're trying to shop smart here, not stop altogether, for heaven's sake. Balance, moderation, rationality. That's what my *Style Strategy* is about. And that's what yours should be about, too.

Fragrance is the only thing that's about your being, your soul, and it's for people size zero to twenty-two and ages twelve to ninety.

MICHAEL KORS

Find ways to control your spending and to channel it in the right direction. Cut out what isn't absolutely necessary and find inexpensive alternatives whenever possible. But *enjoy yourself*. When you're having a bad day and your credit card is burning a hole in your pocket, buy yourself a small treat. A new lipstick in the perfect shade of red, or maybe in a color you've never tried before. Or an ounce of a new fragrance. When I'm completely frazzled at work and know that as soon as I'm done, I'll have to rush home to take care of my family (I love taking care of my family, don't get me wrong, but it can be exhausting), just stopping for a second to spritz myself with a new perfume instantly refreshes me. Every time I catch a whiff of it during the day, it calms me. It's so easy and completely satisfying.

The final step in my *Style Strategy* is all about taking care of yourself. But it's also about keeping your priorities while doing so. It might help to repeat the mantra here!

I will not retire while I've still got my legs and my makeup box.

BETTE DAVIS

You must pamper yourself frequently. It's absolutely vital. After all, to feel good is to look good. And to feel good, it's essential to find a little me-time. It allows you to wind down and take a breather. Recover from your workday; forget the million and one tasks that need doing. At least once a week, I take an hour or two for myself and get a facial (you can do it at home!), or a mani-pedi, or a deep conditioning hair mask, or even something as simple as a nice hot bubble bath. The ritual is just as important as whatever treatment I'm indulging in. Between a career and motherhood, sometimes even just one free hour a week is tough to manage. But you must find a way to carve out this time. We all need to recharge our batteries. You will be a better worker, mother, and friend. *And* nurturing yourself is at the core of realizing your style and projecting it to the world.

STOP AND SMELL THE FLOWERS

So many of life's pleasures aren't about hitting the mall. We all know this. Shopping is great, but you need some soulful exercise as well. Below are some quick and easy things you can do to pamper yourself inexpensively. These simple activities will stimulate your creativity, revitalize your spirit, and save you money in one swoop.

GARDENING: Literally: Stop and smell the flowers, or plant some flowers, or just do some light weeding. Soak up the sun, get back to nature, and *relax*.

WALK: Just walk around the block, find a nice park, breathe fresh air, and everything will seem instantly better. It's the best beauty regimen there is.

NAP: It's impossible to overestimate the importance of sleep. Physically, mentally, and spiritually, it's the cure-all. Even a fifteen-minute catnap will do wonders.

ORDER TAKEOUT AND RENT A MOVIE: Give yourself a break from cooking. Spend a night in enjoying your family's company, or just go it alone. This is chicken soup for the soul.

YOGA: Take a class, breathe deeply, do a downward dog. The results are instant and pure.

The important thing is to take your time
and not get stressed.

DIANE VON FURSTENBERG

The key to pampering yourself on a budget is setting priorities. Isn't that the key to just about everything? Figure out what you don't *really* need, what has an inexpensive substitute, and what is an absolute necessity. We all have one or two (or several) extravagant beauty products that are essential to our arsenal ($70 Cle de Peau concealer, occasional Botox, La Mer skin cream, regular spray tanning, etc.). And it's *OK*. If you do your homework and pare down, you'll be able to justify a few occasional splurges. When it comes right down to it, most of these items have an excellent, inexpensive, and—even better—all-natural counterpart. I can't tell you how much I've spent on skin treatments over the years. I admit it, I'm a sucker for packaging; if it comes in a pretty package, I believe every single promise on the box, no matter how far-fetched. However, when I was pregnant with my son, I decided to try going minimal—just Ivory soap, witch hazel toner, and Aveeno moisturizer (always with sunscreen!). My skin was brighter and healthier in just a few weeks, and it still is. And my bank account is larger. It seems so obvious, that putting as few chemicals as possible on your skin is really good for your complexion. What's good for the environment is good for you, too. Remember that.

So try paring down your beauty regimen and see what works for you. Cut down on your splurges, but don't eliminate them completely. Everything in moderation. A good rule of thumb: Don't buy anything that causes pangs of guilt at the register. Guilt nullifies pampering. And think investment—choose products that will last for a while. Then, every time you indulge, you'll appreciate it all the more.

I'm living so far beyond my income that
we may almost be said to be living apart.

e e cummings

HAIR AND MAKEUP

In my opinion, hair and makeup are as much a part of your wardrobe as clothing and jewelry. Without question, they are integral to defining your personal style. Much like shoes, great hair and makeup can make sweatpants glamorous (Jennifer Lopez, for instance) and bad hair and makeup can make you look like a drag queen, even if you're wearing Chanel. A fantastic haircut adds that little bit of polish to every ensemble and it saves you valuable prep time. It shouldn't take hours to get your hair to look as if you didn't spend any time on it at all. The great thing about a really good cut is that it will grow out nicely and require minimal upkeep—so worth it. Do indulge in a quality cut and color at least twice a year. It's an investment, but you'll be able to easily maintain the look between visits with trims and touch-ups.

FASHION FLASH

GREAT HAIR THAT CHANGED THE WORLD

EDIE SEDGWICK: I love that iconic photo of Edie getting her signature silver boy-cut on a fire escape. Such an original.

MRS. ROBINSON: Anne Bancroft had the sexiest blonde streak in cinema history.

ANNIE LENNOX: Beautiful androgyny.

PRINCESS LEAH: Those buns! We all know them. We all love them.

PAM GRIER: Her Afro inspired so many women to reclaim their cultural heritage. Love her and her hair for sparking such a positive movement.

JENNIFER ANISTON: She may wish it would disappear forever, but the "Rachel" modernized layering and created a sensation in '90s hairstyling.

BRIGITTE BARDOT: Sex kitten with fringy bangs. No one did it better. Flirty and effortless.

DOROTHY HAMILL: She skated like a dream, but that mushroom cut created a generation of humiliating school photos, and it still rears its head on occasion.

BETTIE PAGE: The quintessential pin-up 'do. Legions of women have again flocked toward this hairstyle.

ELVIS: Nobody wore a pompadour like Elvis.

GETTING YOUR HAIR "DID"

Get highlights rather than all-over color; your roots won't show as quickly and you can go longer between touch-ups.

As I said, most beauty products do have excellent inexpensive alternatives, but I really haven't found any low-cost shampoos and treatments that work as well as their higher-priced counterparts. Of course, there is a range, and hair is *so* individual. Find a good shampoo, conditioner, and styling product that you like. Consult your stylist for advice, or ask friends whose hair is similar to yours. And don't go crazy with a million different products; you should be able to get by with just a texturizer or smoother.

An extremely easy way to offset the expense of pricey shampoos is to wash your hair every other day. Especially if you have curly or coarse hair, the drier it is, the less often you need to shampoo. Let your natural oils do what they do. Just rinse when you're in the shower and add a little conditioner to the ends if necessary. It's better for your hair and your scalp, your color will last longer, and your luxurious products will stretch further, too. A no-brainer, if you ask me.

Fortunately, when it comes to cost, cosmetics and skin care products are quite different from hair care products. There's an economical way to replace just about any one of them. Seriously, Ivory soap is the best complexion bar I've ever used.

Your mother probably swore by some old standby cleanser, like Phisoderm or Cetaphil. Most dermatologists agree: The fewer ingredients contained within a product, the better that product is for you. Luckily, fewer ingredients usually equates to a lower price, too. Marilyn Monroe used Vaseline petroleum jelly as a moisturizer, and believe it or not, specialists agree that it is one of the most effective on the market, unless you have very oily skin. (Many, however, will likely find it just a touch heavy.)

TRIAL SIZES ROCK

Look for sample sizes of expensive shampoo, conditioner, and styling products. Most drugstores have them. Ask about them at your salon. It's a perfect way to try different brands to find what you like without spending a fortune and cluttering up your bathroom.

A bit of lusting after someone
does wonders for the skin.

ELIZABETH HURLEY

There are absolutely tons of natural skin rejuve-
nators like honey, yogurt, or oatmeal. Besides their
numerous beneficial qualities, many of these natural alternatives are appealing because they can be
used all over. Jojoba oil is great for your body, hair,
and scalp. I love, love, love multitaskers—they save
money, time, and space! Can you ask for more? I
can't! After your tailor, the Internet is your second
best friend. Look online; there is a plethora of reci-
pes for all-natural facials and hair masques, tons of
suggestions for every skin type. Experiment. Invite
the girls over and ask everyone to bring a homemade
beauty treatment. Think of it as a beauty potluck.
Throw in a chick flick, have some cocktails, give each
other mani-pedis, and relax. Bask in the knowledge
that you are pampering yourself guilt-free and being
eco-friendly at the same time.

EARTH MOTHERS

Try some of these natural treatments. You probably already have all the ingredients in your kitchen, and there's no preparation involved. They're perfect for those of us with hectic schedules. I just love them.

- Wash your face, then dab honey all over, right from the jar, and relax for fifteen minutes. It smells good and it's a great antioxidant. Your skin will be baby-soft, and it reduces redness, too. I was absolutely amazed when I tried it.
- Wash your face, then dab plain, unflavored yogurt all over. It's a natural source of alpha hydroxy acid. Your pores will disappear.
- Before washing your hair, massage jojoba oil into your scalp, put on a cap, and relax for fifteen minutes (multi-task and give yourself a honey facial at the same time). Jojoba removes build-up from your scalp, prevents dandruff, and conditions your hair.

fashion
101

**HISTORY OF
COSMETICS**

- Cosmetics have been around nearly as long as man. There is evidence that the ancient Egyptians (who did eyeliner so well) used cosmetics as early as 4,000 BC.
- At about 1,000 AD, Abu-al-Qasim al-Zahrawi, also known as Abulcasis, wrote a thirty-volume medical encyclopedia called *Al-Tasrif*. He actually dedicated an entire chapter to cosmetics, which he referred to as "medecine of beauty." A translation eventually made its way to the West. Believe it or not, cosmeceuticals have been around for centuries.
- Around 3,000 BCE, the Chinese began to stain their fingernails; they used different colors to represent social status. Ancient manis—who knew?
- And finally, Hollywood brought the makeup obsession to the masses in the twentieth century and forever altered the way we think about great lipstick and the perfectly shaped eyebrow.

CELEBRITIES SHOP AT THE DRUGSTORE, TOO

- GINNIFER GOODWIN: Swears by Rosebud Salve.
- GISELE BÜNDCHEN: Loves Max Factor 2000 Calorie Mascara.
- REESE WITHERSPOON: Uses Johnson & Johnson baby shampoo on her blonde locks.
- LINDSAY PRICE: Keeps her skin smooth with St. Ives Apricot Scrub (a personal favorite of mine).
- NICKY HILTON: Bioré pore strips keep her blackhead-free.
- MARCIA CROSS: Fights wrinkles with Olay Age Defying Daily Renewal Cream.

Drugstore cosmetics have always been a guilty pleasure of mine. Actually, they are a guilt-*free* pleasure because they are so inexpensive! Some of the best eye shadow I have ever owned came in a plastic case of fifty colors, each the shape of a flower petal, and it only cost $9.95. Don't ask what made me even pick it up, let alone buy it. A whim? The pretty colors? Who knows? But they turned out to be excellent shadows. The hues were intense, they went on smoothly, and they lasted all day.

So when you have that urge to buy makeup, any kind of makeup, try out some drugstore bargains. They're fun, and you can play with colors you might not otherwise try. Experimentation keeps you young, it keeps your look fresh, and it exercises your ability to assess what works on you and what doesn't. You have to keep that muscle toned. As soon as you become complacent or too comfortable with what's familiar, you're in danger of becoming dated. Know what flatters you and have your routine down for those times when you need to be flawless and ready to go in ten minutes. But when you're doing

fashion
101

MAKEUP THERAPY

In the '30s, Leonard Lauder coined the term the "Lipstick Index": When the Dow goes down, lipstick sales go up. Women have always cheered themselves up with a little maquillage.

housework or running to the grocery store, break out and try a completely crazy color now and then. Just because. It's a great creative exercise that tests your fashion courage. We all had that teacher in high school who had obviously perfected her makeup routine in 1965 and never gave it another thought. Mine had a perfectly sculpted Dorothy Hamill bob, light-blue eye shadow, and frosty peach lipstick. Great back then. Not so good now, ladies.

Beauty is in the eye of the beholder and it may be necessary from time to time to give a stupid or misinformed beholder a black eye.

MISS PIGGY

Take this pampering seriously. Rejuvenate your beauty regimen. Try new things. Take a hot bubble bath. Enjoy a facial mask while you're making dinner. Your irrational shopping urges will virtually disappear and you will radiate serenity and beauty. Well, at least beauty. Serenity is a little harder to maintain. But looking great is a step in the right direction.

"My fashion is about the urban woman in the year 3000. I think about obscure, weird things and try to create a world around them."

LADY GAGA

CHAPTER
SIX

Fair Trade and Other Tricks

HERE ARE SO MANY WAYS to indulge in luxurious clothing without overspending. Smart shopping is definitely one way. So is creative shopping. Preworn (it
does sound better than "used") clothing is no longer a
fashion faux pas. The patina of a garment with history
is actually attaining a certain status; it makes sense, it's green, and
quite honestly, no one will know it was preworn unless you tell them.

There's a new craze sweeping the nation. Swap Parties. OK,
technically it's not new, but an upscale, modern take on the old-
fashioned swap meet. Invite all of your girlfriends over and ask them
to bring any gently used clothing that they would like to take out of
rotation. Be sure to provide a full-length mirror and a private room
for your modest guests to change in. You can set up different areas
for skirts, dresses, accessories, etc. Make it as formal or as casual as
you want. The only rule is that the garments must be in good condition. Of course, you can make more rules if you like, but try to keep
things simple and relaxed. It's a party, right? Specify only cocktail
dresses or only business clothes, whatever you and your friends may
have and/or want. Items that are only worn on special occasions,

like formal gowns or cocktail dresses, are perfect for a Swap Party. They're usually next to new, you always need one, and no one wants her party dress to be recognizable as her *only* one. How many pairs of shoes or belts are hiding in the back of your closet, lonely and forgotten? If you've been following my instructions you should know exactly how many! Have some drinks and hors d'oeuvres, get dressed up, and swap accessories. Everyone goes home with something they love, and it doesn't cost a dime.

People used to throw rocks at me because of my clothes. Now they wanna know where I buy them.

CYNDI LAUPER

If you need additional guidance, there are an increasing number of resources and magazine articles about planning Swap Parties. Everyone's doing it, and it can be quite chi-chi. Such parties are even garnering corporate sponsors. Visa hosts the VisaSwap in London. Yes, a credit card company is sponsoring the event! And it's not only about saving money, it's also about preserving the environment. Twiggy (that's right, the supermodel) offers a Swap Party planning kit stressing the eco-friendliness of preworn clothing. Leave it to the English! Then follow their example.

Zest is the secret of all beauty.
There is no beauty that is attractive without zest.

CHRISTIAN DIOR

So you've probably noticed that there's a party theme running through this book. It's completely intentional. These days, it's so difficult to make time for yourself, much less for friends. Between work, family, and trying to curb spending, going out with the girls often winds up at the bottom of your priorities list—or off the list completely. But friends are important! And connections are, too. You *need* the emotional support you get from talking, venting, reminiscing, and gossiping. We all do. That alone is therapy and a beauty treatment all in one. Exchanging ideas, networking, borrowing from each other's style, giving fashion advice, getting fashion advice, and staying abreast of the latest sales and shops is essential to your well-being. All of it keeps you fresh and vibrant and in touch. You just might discover that when you and your friends pool your resources, you have what it takes to start your dream business together. Hey, you never know. At the very least, you can give each other moral support and career counseling. You've got to support Team Woman.

Being frugal does not mean you have to stay home alone and deprive yourself. We've grown to equate socializing with going OUT.

Drinks, dinner, maybe the theater. We're talking hundreds of dollars by the end of a fully packed evening. Remember that getting together with friends is about the *friends*; a table at the best restaurant and expensive wine are window dressing. A momentary pleasure. A passing fancy. You need to rethink what truly makes you happy. Appreciate the little things. Take advantage of your community's resources and contribute your resources to the community. Having a strong support system of both family and friends gives you a sense of confidence, of comfort in your own skin. And I can't say it too many times: That's really the core of style.

So I say, any time there's an excuse for a party—make it happen. It's so easy to throw something casual together, and there's no better way to bond with your ladies than over clothes and makeup, and yes, cocktails and hors d'oeuvres.

IN THE KNOW

DRESSFLIX

If you have a fabulously glamorous party to attend and you just have to have that Prada clutch or Gucci dress, and there's absolutely no way you can afford it, consider a rental. Men rent tuxes all the time, right? Do some research in your community and see what's available.

TRENDS

Trends change all the time, and as I've said, you don't want to spend a fortune on them. But luckily, you don't have to. Especially with the increasing (by-the-minute, maybe by-the-second) popularity of guest designers developing limited edition lines for mass retailers. Karl Lagerfeld started the trend with his line for H&M. Since that debut, this innovative retailer has also featured collections from Stella McCartney and Roberto Cavalli, among others. Genius! Target has collaborated with such illustrious names as Alexander McQueen, Tracy Feith, Jovovich-Hawk, and Proenza Schouler. Payless with Abaeté and Christian Siriano. Gap with Pierre Hardy. Urban Outfitters with Lark & Wolff by Steven Alan and byCORPUS. These are just a few of the partnerships that have followed Mr. Lagerfeld's lead. These one-time collaborations are designed to be affordable, up-to-the-minute, and short-lived. They allow everyone a little access to the rarefied world of couture, and I'm all for it.

Designing a one-off collection for H&M is one of the most exciting and innovative ways to introduce my clothes to a broader range of women.

STELLA MCCARTNEY

fashion
101

THE BOOMERANG

EFFECT

Why do we all suddenly need gladiator sandals? Where exactly do trends come from? It's good to apply a little critical thinking here so you won't be seduced so easily. They come from the streets, the textile industry, and the fashion industry. And trends tend to follow the inverse rule: If something is in this season, its opposite will be in next season. Did you notice that just as low-rise jeans couldn't fall any farther below the hips, ultra-high-waist jeans started showing up on the runway?!

If you're attempting to stay ahead, or at least on the cusp of the curve, you may have noticed that trends aren't completely random. They tend to follow necessity. In the '40s, the head wraps that women initially wore to protect their hair while they were working in factories eventually made their way into fashion magazines. Before long, an upscale version was all the rage. At the same time, the shoulder pads in military uniforms became *de rigueur* in women's clothing. They resurfaced in the '80s, during the Cold War, and I've been seeing them on the runways again lately. And my good friend Marc Jacobs revamped the worn jeans and plaid shirts worn by countless '90s slackers into his always visionary haute couture version. In 2000, John Galliano for Christian Dior famously presented his "homeless chic" runway show featuring models in torn clothing and trash bags—a fitting end to the millennium and certainly about as far as it gets from the over-the-top, jewel-encrusted glamour that followed. So if you feel brave enough to try to get ahead of the trends, pay attention to people on the streets and peruse the fashion Web sites to get a sense of what people are wearing around the world. Once you see what's out there in the zeitgeist, subtly, *very* subtly at first, test the waters. Work your vision of fashion's future. You never know, you may just start a style trend yourself.

fashion 101

THE ALL-IN-ONE

In England during World War I (leave it to the English again!), the government attempted to popularize a "National Standard Dress." Cotton and wool were needed for military uniforms, so this dress was made of silk. It had metal buckles instead of a zipper, so it was adjustable. It promoted the idea that every woman could own just one multifunctional dress that would serve as a cocktail, evening, and day dress, as well as a nightgown. Now, I do love multitaskers but there is a limit. Needless to say, it didn't catch on.

Although I don't believe in spending a fortune on fads, I love them as much as the next woman, which is why I am so excited by the growing number of inexpensive but very on-trend European stores that have opened locations here in the United States. Each provides an endless supply of cheap chic. Zara, from Spain, was one of the first, followed by H&M from Sweden, Topshop from England, and UNIQLO from Japan. And there's always the Internet. Globalization is here and it's made affordable fashion much more accessible *and* more stylish. Buy just a few trendy pieces each season and mix them in with your basics. Once they've passed their prime, put them in storage and wait. In a few years, they'll be retro! A smattering of new, fun items will freshen up your old standbys and will help them to last longer. The more rotation you have, the less wear and tear each piece will have to endure.

FABRICS DO MATTER

Go for blends that contain more than 50 percent natural fibers—try to avoid anything that has to be dry cleaned. I generally try to avoid 100-percent synthetics as they tend to pill (I mentioned this earlier, but it bears repeating: Pills are beyond sloppy-looking.)

- Synthetics don't breathe well, and they retain odors— not good!
- 100 percent cotton and wool are wonderful because they look great, come in rich, beautiful colors, are comfortable, inexpensive, easy to care for, they last for a long time, and they're environmentally friendly.

CHEAP THRILLS

OK, this is a good place to stop and review my tips from Chapter Four about how to differentiate between Cheap, Inexpensive, and Bargain items, as well as what constitutes *kitschy* versus *tacky*. Once you've refreshed your memory, follow these guidelines for smart, inexpensive shopping. You'll find that one of the only thrills that may possibly outdo slipping your feet into a new pair of Prada sandals is the thrill of transforming a plain ensemble into a paradigm of fabulousness for under $50.

These cheap thrills are an important component of my *Style Strategy*. They are the window dressing. Mixing high and low fashion is very of-the-moment and, in my opinion, this eclectic approach is here to stay. Remember, your clothes are an expression of *you*, of your individuality. You aren't expressing yourself when you're dressed head to toe in one designer. And really, how can you have fun with fashion when everything you own is a valuable treasure? You should be striving for balance. Playfulness and humor are just as vital to fashion as good taste. Every true fashion icon has managed to blend these aspects flawlessly, from Gwen Stefani to Chloë Sevigny to Natalie Portman. None of these ladies are afraid to mix it up. Sometimes they might make a misstep, but that's just the risk of being a maverick. When these ladies hit it, it's magic.

IN THE KNOW

LAYER IT ON THICK

If an item can be layered, you probably don't need to spend a fortune on it. For instance, I wear most of my tank tops and T-shirts under another tank or a sweater, so I don't need to get too fancy with these. Save your precious dollars for the outer wrapping.

Here are some indispensable tips for dressing up the basics, adding some glitter, and allowing *you* to shine through.

Knits: While good construction is a must for any garment, knits are very forgiving. It's possible for them to look good without much tailoring, and less tailoring means less expense. It also means an easier fit. Knits are your friend as long as you wear them judiciously. They are clingy by nature, so make sure they cling in the right places! Pair an inexpensive pullover with a designer skirt, or wear layered tanks under a jacket. Play with color; you can take more risks when you're spending less money. Fun, inexpensive knit pieces will complement your more refined basics perfectly.

fashion 101

PAPER DOLL

DRESSING

In 1966, the Scott Paper Co. (as in Scott tissue) ran a special promotion for their new Colorful Explosions line of paper napkins, paper towels, and toilet tissue. They offered consumers a chance to buy a paper dress in one of two patterns for just $1.25 each. The dresses were A-line, sleeveless shifts with one front pocket, and were so popular that they spurred a trend that lasted through 1968. In the 1960s, Campbell's Soup also made a paper dress called the Souper, inspired by Andy Warhol.

Moda Mia dresses came in Mexican prints, sold for $2, and had instructions for cutting them down to create different styles. This paper clothing was actually made of Dura-Weve, a combination of wood pulp strengthened with rayon mesh. You can still find these dresses on eBay and some vintage stores. They are surprisingly adorable. It would be pretty spectacular if they were to make a comeback.

Tank Tops and Camisoles: I love, love, love tank tops; it's simply impossible to have too many and, luckily, they're easy to find at a steal. I usually look for 100 percent cotton, although I also like to have a few very lightweight rayon or silk camisoles, too. You can always turn to the old standby: a three pack of Hanes white tanks. I'm guilty of owning far too many.

Tights: Again, you can never have enough of these. Edie Sedgwick famously wore only a leotard and tights to parties; she did have phenomenal legs. Marvelous hosiery is an ideal showcase for superlative gams, although most of us aren't that brave. And there's a reason, few of us have the flair to carry it off. I'm always on the lookout for tights on sale: Spring is the best time to find a bargain, so stock up then for next winter. They are perfect to wear with shorts, skirts, or under trousers for warmth and contouring. We all need to cheat on occasion, especially in the winter. Open weaves, like fishnets or lace, are an instant dress-up for a more casual skirt, and sweater tights are a cozy touch of modesty for a short skirt. Wear them to infuse a dash of color into a neutral ensemble. What more could you ask of an accessory?

However, all stockings are not created equal. Poorly made tights may not even make it through one wearing, or worse, they can be horrendously uncomfortable. I can't think of anything more unpleasant than a pair of scratchy stockings that bag around the knees and whose crotch refuses to stay above mid-thigh level. When in doubt, buy a size larger than you think you need. Opaque tights should be thick and matte, and they should maintain their opacity when stretched. Sheer tights should have good elasticity and even

color with no patchy areas. A nylon/Lycra blend or nylon/cotton blend is best. Because I like to be sure of a stocking's texture before I purchase it, I never buy a brand I am unfamiliar with if it comes in a sealed package. For a little oomph, try layering sheer or open-weave tights over an opaque pair in a contrasting color to create fabulous depth and texture. And doubling up allows you to indulge in the allure of lace hosiery without sacrificing warmth.

Here's my short list of must-have tights. Once you've got these covered, go crazy.

- Black opaque
- Black sheer
- Brown
- Fishnets
- Neutral-colored sweater

IN THE KNOW

PLIÉ . . . PLIÉ . . .

- Dance stores carry extremely durable tights (leotards and legwarmers, too) and the prices are usually quite reasonable.
- Online Scandinavian retailers have incredible sweater tights, unrivaled in their colorful stripes and textures.
- And last but not least, DKNY tights last forever, literally years.

Fitted Tees: These must-haves are perfect for layering and adding a hue of color to an outfit. Stock up on a variety of necklines, colors, and sleeve styles and lengths. Fitted tees are a great look under a jacket for the office or with jeans on the weekend. They show off your curves in a low-key way, and they exude a comfortable, sexy vibe.

COTTON CAMOUFLAGE

Done correctly, layering fitted tees or tanks is an excellent way to disguise a little extra flesh around the middle. It's true! Just be careful that you don't emphasize what you are trying to hide. A good rule of thumb is to put dark over light and avoid excessive bunching.

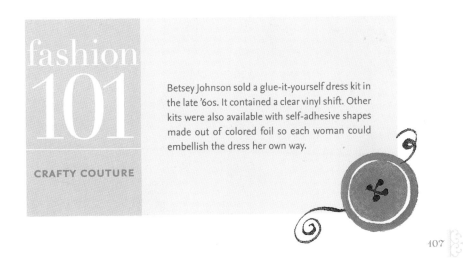

fashion
101

CRAFTY COUTURE

Betsey Johnson sold a glue-it-yourself dress kit in the late '60s. It contained a clear vinyl shift. Other kits were also available with self-adhesive shapes made out of colored foil so each woman could embellish the dress her own way.

Fit is the most neglected aspect of how we dress;
that is, most people wear clothes that are
too big or too small or a combination of both.

TIM GUNN

Skirts: Few things will seem disheveled, make you appear heavier than you are, and generally ruin a look the way a skirt with misplaced darts, crooked seams, puckers, or an ill-fitting waistband does. Darts, in particular, can cause your skirt to pouf in all the wrong places, and pull everywhere else. When correctly executed, darts create a beautifully streamlined effect that actually minimizes bulges, so they're worth some attention. It's challenging (but not impossible) to find an inexpensive skirt that doesn't have at least one of these problems. So, as I said before, *splurge* on a tailored skirt in a solid color with great details: panels, pleats, darts, etc. But do indulge in inexpensive skirts that are flowery, ruffled, or whatever is trendy. Go for fun prints, florals, graphics, metallics, whatever strikes your fancy. Watch out: If the fabric is a cheap synthetic, it probably won't wear well (it's likely to stretch out or be riddled with horrible little pills after only one wear). Purchase these inexpensive skirts at any length except maybe mid-calf— save that for a pencil skirt with a kick pleat.

Casual Dresses: Follow the same rules as for skirts above. Look for tunics, sundresses, or things that you can layer in pretty, flirty fabrics. Because skirts and tops are more versatile than dresses, only the LBD is on my list of basics. I do like to have a few dresses for each season, but I consider them little extras.

fashion 101

GOING GODDESS

During hard times like wars or economic downturns, softness, femininity, and simplicity are desirable. There's something so reassuring about traditional girlishness. Reference beautifully draped floral dresses from the '30s when you're frock shopping.

Accessories: These are a fantastic and utterly simple way to modernize or just add a little zest to your ensemble. You can add a belt (wide, skinny, studded) or a cocktail ring (faux, of course), layer necklaces, stack bangles, or do anything else that strikes your fancy. Use your imagination. Envision new ways to wear old accessories. Cameron Diaz wore a Fred Leighton necklace as a belt with her Emanuel Ungaro gown at the 2002 Oscar Awards; it created quite a sensation. In a good way! Fashion writers gushed over her inventiveness and celebrities have followed her lead ever since.

Use your mother's old clip-on earrings as a brooch—they adorn a neckline beautifully—or clip them to the top of flats as a shoe ornament. I sometimes dress up a plain neckline with glittery hair clips; it's cute jewelry, and I always have backup in case of a hair emergency.

The ways to wear a scarf are infinite. The only limit is your creativity. You can wear a scarf as a head wrap, a belt, a sarong, around your neck, short and neat, ascot style, as a bandanna, long and flowing, with fringe, without fringe, patterned, plain, wool, silk, cotton, hand-knit, or over a bouffant. The list goes on and on. Scarves really are among the most versatile accessories.

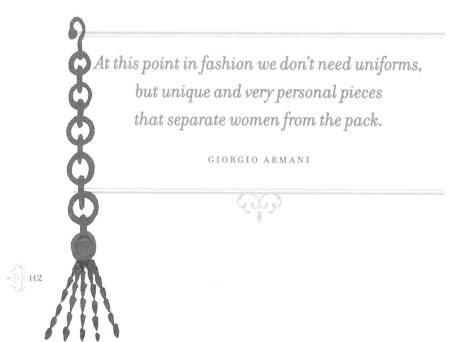

fashion
101

SLUMDOG
MILLIONAIRESS

Alicia Keys wore a sari-style silk wrap over a white tank and jeans to the 2002 Grammys. Her look was glamorized street; it was universally deemed unique, chic, and worldly.

So revel in your cheap thrills. Go for the kitsch factor. A d o r n your basics. They're looking a little less basic already, aren't they? Remember balance. And if you have a fashion "don't" one day, accept that it's not the end of the world. Learn from it. It's better to try and fail than to have never tried at all.

At this point in fashion we don't need uniforms, but unique and very personal pieces that separate women from the pack.

GIORGIO ARMANI

INDIE LABELS

Finding a new independent designer is always a treat. You almost don't want to let anyone else know about your hidden treasure. The clothes are often priced a little lower than their more established counterparts and they tend to be more unique and a little funkier. The Internet has given everyone unprecedented access to what the smaller labels have to offer, and if you are a savvy shopper you may even manage to get ahead of the crowd. I am always on the lookout for new discoveries, and there's nothing more satisfying than the smug knowledge that you won't see anyone else in the exact same thing. Of course, if you put your outfits together skillfully enough, your look will be unique just by virtue of the way you wear it. And that, ladies, is true style.

MULTICULTI SHOPPING

I never pass up an opportunity to check out small ethnic boutiques or markets. Many times these little stores are a mélange of specialty foods, books, accessories, and clothing. Like anything else, you don't want to dress head-to-toe in any one national costume (unless it's yours), but adding some Indian bangles, African print scarves, or a Chinese silk shirt here and there lends a bit of exotic flair to an otherwise basic ensemble. Whenever you are in a city that has a Chinatown, or other neighborhood that is home to a particular culture or population, be sure to shop there. There are usually great bargains to be had because the merchandise isn't marketed as an exotic import; it's a part of the community's heritage, included in their everyday staples—and it's usually very well made, or even better, handmade.

THE GLOBAL VILLAGE

The fashion industry has a long tradition of adopting styles from around the world and incorporating them into their designs. Pay attention to what people in other places are wearing via any form of global media (TV, films, magazines, the Web) and you are sure to be inspired by something you see. Here are some of my favorite examples.

- KILTS: Schoolgirls, New England preppies, and brave men alike sport this Scottish classic with flair.

- BINDIS: Gwen Stefani gave us her Western take on this South Asian symbol. This bit of sparkle between your eyebrows represents the sixth chakra, or the seat of "concealed wisdom."

- MOCCASINS: This Native American footwear never fully goes out of style, whether it is a boot, slip-on, or sandal.

- HENNA: The South Asian nations have a beautiful history of body decoration. Madonna and Prince are just two of the many trendsetters who brought this art to the West. Not only is it subtly graceful, henna art is traditionally used for celebrations and important occasions.

- PASHMINA: Everyone should own at least one of these luxurious Persian cashmere shawls. They're lightweight, so warm, and so chic.

- MIDDLE EASTERN SCARVES: Everyone is wearing them again (echoing an '80s trend). There is a reason these fabulous scarves cycle back into vogue every couple of decades or so: They're so versatile.

- HAREM PANTS: They're back! These amazingly comfortable pants are based on traditional Indian attire and add a little spice to your look.
- AMERINDIAN DRESS: These beautiful, hand-embroidered frocks have become a summer classic in Europe and the United States. They originated with the indigenous cultures of South America.

AVOID THE TOURIST TRAP

Whenever you travel to a country that is known for textiles or ceramics or some other craft, be adventurous and search for the little places off the beaten path that are not aimed at tourists and you will come home with a year's worth of inexpensive and gorgeous accessories, as well as an endless supply of fabulous gifts for your friends.

These are but a few of the shopping tricks I use in my life. I urge you to think about your shopping habits, use the tips in this book, discover your own, and share them with friends. There are no limitations on how to shop smart. Identify what works for you and truly embrace the strategy and creativity behind saving money and feeling and looking your very, very best.

"Style is knowing who you are, what you want to say, and not giving a damn."

GORE VIDAL

The Luxe Life

A H, LUXURY! Who doesn't want to feel it, live it, wear it? And much like pampering yourself when you absolutely need to, owning a few luxe pieces is a good idea if you can swing it. When economizing, you don't have to forgo extravagant labels entirely. You just need to do your homework and be patient. There are quite a few different ways to obtain high-end fashion at a deep discount.

Don't ever forget that knowing when to give yourself a pat on the back is key in all areas of life. Don't be too hard on yourself if you splurge on something you've decided you can't live without. Enjoy the new purchase, reset your priorities, go through my *Style Strategy* checklist again, and repeat the mantra. **Shop smart, stay chic, and make it last.**

FASHION FLASH

MOVIE MANIA

SHOPPING SCENES THAT KILLED

- We all remember the hooker with a heart of gold montage on Rodeo Drive in *Pretty Woman*.
- And what about the cult '80s zombie movie, *Night of the Comet*? I love it when, right after the meteor hits, the sisters go to the deserted mall and try on all of the clothes before they are forced to fight off the undead.
- Of course, every episode of *Sex and the City*.

SAMPLE SALES

An excellent way to go luxe without breaking the bank is to hit up a sample sale. This is an event where designers sell samples from their line that have either been worn by models or are overstock items. Traditionally, these sales have taken place primarily in cities that are home to the fashion industry, such as New York and Los Angeles. At one time they were strictly advertised through private mailing lists and industry publications, so only die-hard fashionistas could take advantage of them. Now, with the greater number of indie labels, Web sites, and blogs devoted to fashion, these events are far more accessible. And if you don't happen to live where they occur, you can still find them online.

If you are planning to travel to a big city, I highly recommend that you do your homework and find out if there are going to be any sample sales while you are there. Nothing compares to the experience of throwing yourself into the fray and fighting for these unrivaled bargains in person. Bring cash and don't be surprised if there are no dressing rooms. It's total madness, but if you're in the right frame of mind, and you are able to just go with it, you'll emerge with some absolutely fabulous pieces.

OUTLET MALLS

You've got to love an outlet mall. Everyone does. It's definitely a day trip, since these shopping extravaganzas have become so enormous, but there are so many fantastic deals to be found when you discover a really good one. You can even plan a "girls" vacation to visit different outlets around the country. Talk about an incentive to get to your next destination.

We all know you can find amazing deals on name brands at outlet stores, but why? How did outlet stores come to be? It's actually a fairly recent phenomenon.

An outlet is a retail store that sells manufacturer rejects, irregulars, samples, and overstock of clothes that regular retailers are not able to sell. Harold Alfond, founder of the Dexter Shoe Company, is often credited with creating the first outlet store. Rather than selling his factory-damaged shoes at a steep discount to a reseller who would give them a significant markup, he decided to take matters into his own hands. In the 1960s, he opened a store called Dexter's Skowhegan Factory, where he sold his imperfect shoes directly to the public. Even though he offered deeply discounted prices, the business was incredibly profitable.

And thus the outlet store was born, quickly followed by the outlet mall: a cornucopia of high-end brands at low-end prices, all in one place.

First and foremost, I wear what I love.

MICHELLE OBAMA

VINTAGE AND CONSIGNMENT SHOPS

I'm sure you've noticed that there is more and more vintage on the red carpet these days. Preworn is here to stay. Of course, this means that you are less likely to find a mint classic Halston for $10 at your local Salvation Army. But there are still bargains to be had, and vintage clothing, especially anything made pre–1970, usually has much more complex tailoring and finishing than today's clothes do. In other words, they're not as mass-produced, so even the more commercial labels of that era are better made, last far longer, and have some really exquisite details. Look for garments that are lined, structured, and don't look too specifically of their time. Mix a '50s floral sundress that has a fitted bodice and full skirt with a contemporary bag, shoes, and jewelry. It's fresh, amazing, and stylish, stylish, stylish.

If vintage isn't your thing, consignment shops are a lovely alternative. They are everywhere, and just like any boutique, each one has a different flavor, so you need to shop around and see which stores have clothes that you like. Check in with them frequently—that's the key to nabbing those hidden treasures. It's almost impossible to find what you want when you have a specific piece in mind, but if you browse them regularly you never know what will turn up.

VINTAGE SHOPPING

Always remember: Not only is vintage shopping a fabulous way to find unique and sophisticated clothes, it's also eco-friendly. These are some of the best vintage detinations throughout the United States. If you're ever in any of these cities, you must check out at least one. Or all of them. You won't be disappointed.

NEW YORK

The Family Jewels: A preferred destination for photographers, stylists, movie studios, celebrities, and fashionistas, this extraordinary shop carries vintage pieces from the turn of the century through the '80s. Love it.

New York Vintage: You must see this amazing selection of couture and high-end designer clothing and accessories. *And* they have an on-site tailor. Perfection.

What Comes Around Goes Around: This shop carries a marvelous combination of high-end vintage pieces and contemporary labels (including their own eponymous line). You can shop at this industry favorite online or in their NY and LA boutiques.

LOS ANGELES

Decades and Decades Two: Decades is the source of many a red-carpet splash. They have beautiful twentieth-century couture and accessories. Its sister boutique, Decades Two, offers a unique selection of high-end consignment pieces from the '90s to the present. And this being Hollywood, you can imagine the number of celebrity consignors.

ReVamp Vintage: The proprietress of this great little shop offers limited-edition collections of vintage-inspired clothing, focusing on items from the 1910s through the 1950s. They also carry great accessories.

Shareen Vintage: This bicoastal shop (locations in NY and LA) is a treasure trove of moderately priced, and absolutely fabulous, vintage styles. Every third Saturday of the month Shareen has a huge sale. It's a must-go.

The Way We Wore: From the Victorian era through the '80s, this boutique has a great selection of women's vintage in a range of prices.

LAS VEGAS

The Attic: This unbelievably enormous warehouse of vintage extravagance bills itself as the biggest vintage collection in the world. Can you expect any less from Las Vegas? The prices are reasonable, the selection is phenomenal, they offer their own line of custom designs, and they do their part for the environment by turning unsalvagable garments into rags (which they sell in bulk). Reduce, Reuse, Recycle!

Fruition: If you're looking for upscale '80s and '90s (I'm still upset that this is considered vintage) hip-hop gear, this is the place. But be prepared to drop some cash.

Refinery Celebrity Resale Boutique: The name says it all. Very high-end consignment.

Valentino's Zootsuit Connection: You can find '40s and '50s gabardine as well as great high-end vintage clothes and accessories here.

MIAMI

Donovan & Gray: This Miami boutique has wonderful vintage clothing and accessories.

GLAM! Vintage: This little shop has a fabulous selection of clothing and tons of reasonably priced jewelry.

Sasparilla Village: This store is required shopping for vintage designer clothes at great prices.

DALLAS

Ahab Bowen: Fashionistas and designers never miss an opportunity to check out the selection when they're in Dallas.

Dolly Python: You will find an eclectic array of great vintage and up-and-coming designer pieces here.

CHICAGO

Eskell: A glorious mélange of the owner's own eclectic line, hard to find labels, and carefully selected vintage.

Lulu's at the Belle Kay: Old Hollywood glamour is alive and fabulous in this very girly and very spectacular shop.

Viva Vintage Clothing: This boutique is a costume designer's heaven.

Yellow Jacket: So much shopping to do, so little time.

TIPS FROM TWO OF
PROJECT RUNWAY'S FINEST!

There are few things better than getting advice from people you admire. Legendary designer and fellow Project Runway judge Michael Kors and Project Runway season four standout winner Christian Siriano are two wildly creative minds I admire tremendously. Each has a vastly different perspective than the other: Michael having so much experience and long-term success, and Christian looking very much like he's on his way to accomplishing so much (he has already!). I asked each ten questions about shopping, what some of their favorite items are at a bargain, and a few other things I always wondered about. Their answers may surprise and inspire.

MICHAEL KORS

1. List five of your favorite fashion items priced below $50.
   Black T-shirts, white ribbed tanks, rubber flip-flops, cotton bandannas, canvas web army belts.

2. List five of your favorite beauty items priced below $20.
   ChapStick Classic Cherry lip balm, Ivory soap, Jergens Natural Glow moisturizer, John Frieda Beach Blonde spray.

3. How do you decide when to get rid of something in your wardrobe?

    When it's not close to being the right size, skip it. It will never be perfect.

4. What is your favorite store for bargain shopping?

    Kaufman's Army and Navy store, West Forty-second Street, NYC.

5. What is the best fashion advice you've ever heard and who gave it to you?

    "Buy quality; it stands the test of time." My grandfather lived by it.

6. What is your quick pick-me-up for a tired outfit?

    An oversized muffler tied at the neck equals instant glamour.

7. What is your favorite fashion Web site for shopping, fashion tips, etc.?

    MichaelKors.com of course!!

8. What was one piece of clothing you wore that, in retrospect, you consider a fashion "don't"?

    As a teenage fashion student I wore leg warmers and boots. Definitely a don't for men.

9. What fashion "don't" do you see on the streets that particularly bothers you?
    Anyone bigger than Kate Moss shouldn't be wearing short-shorts or hot pants anywhere on a city street.

10. If you could pick one fashion icon to be for one day, who would it be? And why?
    Steve McQueen. He managed to look elegant and chic, but always relaxed and unstudied at the same time.

CHRISTIAN SIRIANO

1. List five of your favorite fashion items priced below $50.
    - UNIQLO printed T-shirt
    - Great pair of guest designer shoes at Payless
    - Accessories each season at H&M: bags and scarves
    - Cashmere socks at Barneys
    - Belts and sunglasses at Zara

2. List five of your favorite beauty items priced below $20.
    - MAC Studio Finish
    - Aveda Hand Relief

- Cibu Take Out shampoo
- Victoria's Secret Very Sexy mascara
- Blistex (it's the best—don't judge!)

3. **How do you decide when to get rid of something in your wardrobe?**
   I get rid of it usually if it has lost the fit. If the denim is not tight, or if my sweater's sleeves are all stretched out. I hate that it has to go!

4. **What is your favorite store for bargain shopping?**
   I think finding designer markdowns is a bit tough. But Filene's Basement, T.J. Maxx, Marshalls—all are still great for bargains on designer brands!

5. **What is the best fashion advice you've ever heard and who gave it to you?**
   Wow, I think the best fashion advice was from two people. I think they were more for the everyday woman, not specific to me, but: Heidi Klum told me that women have to be sexy and chic while they are young; don't wait. And Victoria Beckham told me that heels can never be too high!

6. **What is your quick pick-me-up for a tired outfit?**
   It the outfit is tired, then you need a shoe with a great print or in metallic leather, etc. I also think a huge oversized bag always hides an ugly pair of jeans!

7. What is your favorite fashion Web site for shopping, fashion tips, etc.?

I love so many sites! Gilt.com, Topshop.com, Saks. com, Net-a-porter.com. Oh, and of course, Christianvsiriano.com!

8. What was one piece of clothing you wore that, in retrospect, you consider a fashion "don't"?

I was totally in love with these amazing Donald J [Pliner] pony skin cowboy boots. I always thought they were just so fabulous— actually they are really funny and a mess!

9. What fashion "don't" do you see on the street that particularly bothers you?

I see so many "don't's." It's hard to pick just one. I see color all over the place, but it's always that mustard yellow that only works on some skin tones. Color choices are hard, but when done right are *oh so fab!*

10. If you could pick one fashion icon to be for one day, who would it be? And why?

Wow, who would I be? I would be Mary-Kate Olsen. Oh yes, that would be so interesting, to see how I would choose my outfit each day. I'm sure I would have the pick out of the most random pieces from some of the most amazing designers. It would be like shopping in a department store!

"No material must lie idle, so be a magician and turn old clothes into new."

FROM *MAKE DO AND MEND*,
A PAMPHLET PUBLISHED BY
ENGLAND'S MINISTRY OF INDUSTRY
DURING WORLD WAR II

CHAPTER

EIGHT

Make Do and Mend

Y OU'VE CLEANED YOUR CLOSET, made your lists, learned to shop smart, and now you have an opportunity to exercise your creativity a little more. Remember that "fix-it" pile? As the saying goes, God is in the details. This definitely applies when inspecting the garments that actually have a chance to not only survive your fashion cleansing, but thrive and be worn with pride. Here are some guidelines for assessing some of your wardrobe staples. These tips will help you visualize the possibilities. Every garment has a path, and it's up to you to push it along toward its ultimate, spectacular destiny.

Trousers: It's all about length, length, length. Too long? Too short? You decide. Also, are the cuffs or knees worn? Would they be cuter as a pair of shorts or capris than they are as trousers? Think hard about this. Trousers can be shortened, the legs tapered, and pockets sewn closed to create a sleeker line. The choice you make can result in a brand new look for you *and* a brand new life for your garment.

Skirts: These change with the times, as we all know. Hemlines are always in flux. Going shorter is an easy fix. A mini is sexy, if you have the stems to pull it off. But you can also add a panel of a complementary fabric to the bottom of the skirt to make it longer, giving an older skirt a new, sophisticated line. Think Hepburn—Audrey or Katherine. They both dressed fabulously. These little alterations can add wonderful depth and character to an old skirt that you thought you'd never wear again.

Shirts: Admittedly, these tops are very tricky. You can remove the collar, shorten or remove the sleeves, but a very tailored shirt is complicated to alter. Often it's not worth the trouble unless it's truly a one-of-a-kind piece. If it isn't, think about recycling the fabric for other purposes or giving it a new home.

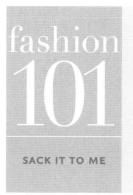

fashion 101

SACK IT TO ME

Need I say more?

When women couldn't afford fabric during the Great Depression, they made dresses out of flour sacks. This was so common that the flour companies began to design the sacks with different prints to appeal to women. The different prints were so identifiable that they became trends.

Dresses: Oh, the possibilities! You can update a dress by shortening the hem, changing the sleeves from long to short or sleeveless, altering the neckline, or by removing or adding embellishments like bows, belts, pockets, ruffles, or even lace. Just as you've done with your skirts, you can lengthen a dress by adding a panel to the bottom. Try adding the same fabric at the neckline too, or use it to make a belt. No one will ever know it wasn't part of the dress's original design. If you love the material, but want something more casual, simply have the bodice removed, add a waistband and *voilà*, your old frock has been instantly transformed into a skirt. Be creative, and channel your inner designer.

Jackets: Blazers are timeless. A perfectly tailored blazer with elbow patches is a "shabby chic" classic. A good tailor can take in a loose-fitting jacket to create a more sophisticated, dressy look. You can also replace the buttons for an easy, yet wholly transformative, makeover. Be sure the buttons will fit through the buttonholes and are big enough to keep the jacket closed. (I know it seems obvious, but the best of us have made this mistake.) Try finding buttons in a contrasting color, too; you will be amazed at the difference!

Sweaters: It's tricky to alter the shape and length of most sweaters because they unravel easily, but again, replacing the buttons on pieces like cardigans can create a whole new look. Unless you want to tie a sweater around your head like a turban as if you just stepped out of *Grey Gardens* (and more power to you, if you dare!), there really isn't much else you can do to alter the sweater itself.

Momma sewed the rags together
Sewin' every piece with love
She made my coat of many colors
That I was so proud of

DOLLY PARTON, "COAT OF MANY COLORS," 1971

fashion
101

**WHERE THERE'S
A WILL,
THERE'S A WAY**

In World War II, ingenious ladies who couldn't find lace or tulle used gauze bandages for additional trimming on dresses and skirts. They even used bandages to make tutus.

Coats: I have a love affair with coats. You can completely refurbish a coat by shortening the sleeves or changing the length. Your indispensable tailor can reshape the collar, embellish it, or even replace it with a fur piece (I advocate faux) to really dress it up. And, yes, replace the buttons. Never underestimate the power of hope and change that button replacement therapy imparts on a garment. New buttons are the Barack Obama of garment renewal. Yes, we can!

Garment renovations often appear to be tricky affairs. What happens when you're looking to do something complicated or difficult, and the solution is not as obvious as you'd hoped? In those cases, consult your tailor. However, there are many ways to accomplish easy and dramatic fixes all by yourself. Sure, not all of us can sew or mend, but when you really want to save something from the recycling pile, you have to give it the ol' college try.

Adding pockets to a garment may not necessarily come to mind as a method of saving your beloved clothes. But keep this in mind: It is a simple way to cover an unfixable hole or stain. You can always use the extra fabric taken from shortening a garment's hem to make a new pocket.

fashion
101

THE GENDER

BENDS

During World War II, women's magazines printed patterns for turning a man's suit into a smart skirt and ladies' jacket. The trousers were transformed into a skirt by ripping the inseam, cutting the legs short, and using the extra material to create a panel. *Voilà!* An A-line skirt. The jacket required just a little shortening of the sleeves and hem to become a flattering ladies' version.

FASHION FLASH

PRETTY IN PINK

Pretty in Pink is one of my favorite makeover movies. I couldn't wait to see how Molly Ringwald's character—the beautiful, funky, independent girl from the wrong side of the tracks, who couldn't afford a new prom gown—would reconstruct a vintage '50s prom dress. The requisite teen movie montage of Molly holding up each piece of the dress, then sewing and resewing, was mesmerizing to me. Although I was a bit disappointed with the final result—a strangely shapeless, pink taffeta column, that movie inspired me to appreciate a beautiful dress and see its possibilities.

The same goes for removing already existing pockets. The fashion gods giveth, but they can also taketh away. Again, perhaps not the most obvious choice for repair, but one that is incredibly effective. Just make sure the color underneath the removed pocket matches the surrounding fabric. The underlying patch of fabric is often less faded and may look completely out of place if exposed. Total no-no.

And then there's adding trim, ruffles, or lace. Goth-ing up a garment with ruffles or lace trim instantly gives it a sexy bohemian look that is great for a night at the theater or a romantic dinner. Very Vampire Chic.

The *Twilight* look isn't for everyone, though, and in that case it's just as easy to *remove* existing trim, ruffles, or lace. Sometimes simplifying an ornate blouse or dress is all it takes to create a classic.

MAKE IT LAST

It is of the utmost importance that you take excellent care of your clothes and shoes. It takes a little extra time, but is *so* worth it. It's absolutely tragic when you have to part with a favorite pair of shoes or a beloved coat too soon. You don't need to take these extra measures with your inexpensive things, but anything that's an investment requires a certain amount of TLC. Lavish your garment with love and attention, and it will be loyal forever.

fashion 101

READ THE LABEL!

Manufacturers began sewing care instructions into clothing during WWII (the golden age of economizing) precisely because proper care makes an enormous difference in the longevity of your garments.

WASHING

Don't wash your garments too frequently. Doing so actually puts a lot of wear and tear on your clothes. Of course, you don't want to walk around in dirty, smelly things, but it isn't necessary to put everything in the machine each time it is worn. Be especially prudent with delicate, stretchy, or intensely colored fabrics. And always, always read the care label.

- Always turn your dark-rinse jeans inside out before washing and keep like colors together.
- Use lingerie bags for sweaters, undergarments, stockings, tank tops, and any delicate knits. Of course, hand washing is the best way to clean your delicates, but who has time for that? I don't. A lingerie bag, mild detergent, the gentle cycle on your machine, and cold water should suffice.
- Always dry knits and delicates flat.
- And finally, air dry whenever possible. This avoids shrinking, helps your stretch fabrics hold their stretch (Lycra actually expands in the dryer), keeps colors fresh, and conserves energy. It's really quite fabulous that one of the greatest side effects of paying attention to your budget involves being more green.

SAVE YOUR SHOES

Don't wear the same pair of shoes every day. Alternating pairs allows shoes time to dry between wearing, which makes them last much longer. Even if they aren't wet on the outside, your feet do produce moisture. An unpleasant thought, but hey, we're all human, and sometimes our feet cry, too.

SHOE CARE

Proper maintenance will add years to the life of your shoes. Here are a few rules to live by.

- Don't wear the same pair every day (as previously discussed).
- Apply a sealant or clear polish to new shoes to protect them from the elements.
- Put heel savers on your shoes *before* they are worn down. If you wait too long, the heels and soles will no longer be fixable.
- Keep them clean; gently brush off dirt before you put them away.
- Use shoe trees to preserve your shoes' shape and always store knee-high boots fully zipped.

- In the winter, if you live in a colder climate where it snows and salt is routinely scattered on walkways, be sure to wipe down shoes or boots with a soft, moist rag after you return from outdoors. Salt *destroys* shoes (nothing cracks leather faster). If your footwear is indeed made of leather, you can also use a small amount of very mild soap, but never do so on rubber. Lastly, don't put shoe trees into wet or damp shoes and never dry them with heat.

THERE'S SOMETHING ABOUT SUEDE

Suede is gorgeous and so luxe, but it doesn't wear as well as smooth leather. It requires more care and maintenance, and once suede starts looking worn, there's no going back. It's not the best choice if you want shoes that will last.

MENDING

Inspect your clothing regularly for snags, holes, stains, etc. Try to catch these little problems before garments are put into the washing machine so they don't become big problems later. And really, there's nothing worse than discovering these mishaps in the middle of a workday. Save yourself the stress. The sooner you take care of these little problems, the easier it is to fix them and avert disaster.

When in doubt, consult your tailor. Mending an article of clothing is almost always less expensive than replacing it, even if you must enlist the help of a professional.

IN THE KNOW

WIRED

Channel your inner Joan Crawford (we all have one): "No wire hangers!" They are terrible for your clothes. Wire hangers ruin the shape of shoulders by stretching them into unsightly points that over time are very difficult to get rid of.

STORAGE

Never, never, never put anything away for the season without having it cleaned first. Always dry clean your winter coats before storing them, even if it doesn't seem like they need it. Coats are exposed to the elements all winter, so when they are packed away without being properly cleaned, the remaining dirt eats away at the fibers. The same goes for sweaters and jackets. They should be folded neatly and kept in clean, airtight containers. Never use hangers for knits; they should always be stored flat.

With all of this advice you can now pamper yourself, pamper your clothing, spend time with friends, and splurge occasionally. If you repeat your mantra daily, it is so easy to rein in your spending without feeling deprived. It is also exciting to discover your personal style—and even more exciting to wear that style out on the town. Learn to play with your look. Have fun. Don't take it too seriously. Your style really should be a natural projection of your inner diva.

fashion 101

TRUE COLLARS

When Richard Nixon was still a young congressman, he and his wife Pat lived on a tight budget. Later, Pat proudly described turning the future president's collars inside out and resewing them to his shirts to make them last longer (The "ring around the collar" is hidden when one does this.)

Parting Words . . .

Beautiful is all I see
when I look at me

THE GO-GO'S, "BEAUTIFUL," 1981

NOW THAT I'VE GUIDED YOU through my personal *Style Strategy*, and let you in on (almost) all of my shopping secrets, you're ready to take off and become the most creative, eco-friendly, fully sustainable, self-reliant, fabulous recessionista diva out there. I strive to make the world a more fabulous place, one reader at a time. And I strive to help every woman realize her own potential. I don't believe in dictating style; I believe in giving you the tools to discover what it is that *you* bring to the table and how you can dress that special something up so you can truly shine.

We are embarking on a new era of self-awareness and sense of community and responsibility. Learning to make the most of your wardrobe and beauty routine are the most obvious elements of personal style, but true style entails marching to the beat of your own drummer, and really enjoying it. Remember that fashion is fun. Live your life, indulge, appreciate your friends and family, and throw impromptu parties whenever possible.

Feel good about yourself, and style will radiate from within you.

Nina

Resources

IF I WROTE DOWN all of the millions of shopping destinations and style resources out there, the list would fill an entire book of its own. So here's a smattering of sites and shops I love. Do your homework, explore, and be sure to check out links on the sites that *you* love. The selection is constantly changing. Remember, ladies: *Shop smart, stay chic, and make it last.*

Enjoy!

SHOPPING

HIGH-END (BARGAINS)

Bluefly.com
At this popular online retailer, you will find a spectacular selection of high-end fashion, usually discounted more than 40 percent.

Century 21
Another NYC legend, this retailer has locations in the tri-state area only, and tragically offers no online shopping. But they do have huge discounts on very high-end labels. It can be a bit of a madhouse, but it's so worth the chaos.

Daffy's

Daffy's is a discount department store with amazing deals on designer labels. Stupendous for lingerie and hosiery. Sadly, this New York original has locations only in New York and New Jersey and does not offer online shopping. But don't miss it on your next visit to NYC.

Gilt.com

You have to become a member to enjoy this site's invitation-only online sample sales. But the good news is that membership is free!

Net-a-Porter.com

If Christian Siriano loves this site, I do, too. And so should you. Smart luxury shopping laid out like an online high-fashion magazine. This site is addictive.

OutletBound.com

This is the definitive guide to outlet shopping—everything about malls, stores, etc.

RevolveClothing.com

This site is not just a fabulous retailer with a great selection of designers. It is also a blog and an online magazine, and it provides a ton of great style advice and editorials.

INDIE LABELS

EspadrillesEtc.com
Browsing this sunny Web site is like taking a vacation in Spain—where these scrumptious espadrilles are made. Everything is gorgeous, gorgeous, and gorgeous. And not too pricey.

MelissaPlasticDreams.com
These amazing plastic shoes are made in Brazil and are more like works of art than footwear. They're completely green, recyclable, cruelty-free, and designed in partnership with numerous illustrious designers. Vivienne Westwood's line is phenomenal. And the Web site is so much fun. I'm gushing, I know.

Shopflick.com
Don't miss this video-powered marketplace for indie-inspired goods. Definitely on the cutting edge.

Sodafine.com
This eclectic Brooklyn boutique carries a unique variety of indie designers and handmade gifts and accessories. Their look is fresh, they carry great dresses, and they feature lots of local talent.

Soiakyo.com
Want to find spectacular trenches and leather jackets? Based in Montreal, Soiakyo makes some of the best coats out there. Even if you aren't shopping for a trench coat, check these out to see some perfect examples of what great buttons can do for a garment.

Tulle4us.com

This indie label offers smashing retro-inspired designs in gorgeous fabrics. Really pretty, feminine pieces, and so reasonably priced.

YourSlipIsShowing.com

Adorable slips with embellished hemlines that are gorgeous enough to wear on their own. There's nothing more glamorous than a hint of velvet, sequins, or feathers peeking out from beneath your hemline. It's such an ingenious way to refurbish skirts and dresses.

INEXPENSIVE AND TRENDS

Forever 21

This chain carries all of the trends. It's the ultimate throwaway chic. And you can find accessories galore.

Gap

Their collaboration with design students from the Rhode Island School of Design to customize the traditional cardigan was an exciting prospect. Rely on them for denim and T-shirts, and also look for great underwear sales online.

H&M

I adore this store. It brings us fashion from Sweden and is inexpensive and great for trends. The merchandise turns over frequently, so there is always something new here. *And* they collaborate with fabulous guest designers. It's an especially great place for tanks in *tons* of colors. Unfortunately, there's no online shopping.

J.Crew

This store is an American classic. J.Crew sponsored the first season of *Project Runway* and they're back in the news thanks to our spectacular, fashion-forward first lady, Michelle Obama.

Madewell1937.com

J.Crew's casual cousin offers a great array of rustic chic looks.

Mango

This international boutique based in Spain carries clothes and accessories that are adorable and contemporary. Their prices are great and they feature wonderful guest designers, too. They have several locations in the United States and comprehensive online shopping. An excellent choice when you want to make fun additions to your basics.

Topshop

There's a reason the English love this store. And now we have location in New York City, too. They also have an American version of their Web site that's wonderful! Affordable, chic, and trendy—it's the whole package.

UNIQLO

A really fun place to find Japanese sportswear. You can shop online or at their store in New York City (of course.).

Urban Outfitters

You can always find good mid-range trends and some really nice indie labels at this youthful chain. And they've jumped on the guest designer bandwagon with some fresh, young, limited-edition lines. There are some real steals on the clearance rack and even more bargains on their Web site.

Victoria's Secret
We're all well acquainted with this unrivaled lingerie store. My good friend, the incomparable Heidi Klum, has worked with them for years. They have fabulous in-store sales, and you can find even deeper discounts online.

Zappos.com
Every shoe under the sun can be found here. If you see a shoe you love in a store, check this Web site before you buy it. You're likely to get a better price. And they're branching out into clothing and accessories, so the shopping will only get better.

Zara
One of the first retailers to offer low-cost versions of high-end designs, this Spain-based chain famously has two-week turnarounds from concept to product. As both an online *and* brick-and-mortar contender, everyone can partake in the bounty.

CHEAP THRILLS

eBay
People have become such insanely savvy eBay shoppers that there aren't nearly as many bargains here as there used to be. But if you have something specific in mind (and a little patience), you never know.

Old Navy

Gap's casual cousin, this retailer is ideal for tanks and sundresses. I love their clearance racks and summer footwear.

Payless

Our own Christian Siriano and other fabulous designers are doing lines for this inexpensive shoe retailer. Payless is back on the map.

Rainbow

This large U.S. chain was founded in 1935, and they are still remarkably inexpensive. If you're looking for young urban wear or plus sizes, you'll find a great selection of trends. And did I mention that they're extremely inexpensive? The clothes are colorful and youthful and many items are 100 percent cotton. Perfect.

Target

Do I even need to describe this one? Second only to the amazing bargains on their sales racks are their amazing guest designers. Target was one of the first big retailers to feature high-end designers at affordable prices. Also, I love their selection of bags and sandals. It's *so* easy to put an outfit together from their constantly updated seasonal merchandise. Target, *très chic!*

T.J. Maxx

I always check for hosiery and denim here. You should too.

ACCESSORIES

Badshannon.com

This quirky silver jewelry is a real find. I adore the meat charm bracelet and the ant bracelet. Believe it or not, the pieces are really feminine and pretty—but with a twist.

Brooks Brothers

Not only do they carry timeless apparel, but you must check out their online scarf tutorial. (That's why I've put them here in the Accessories section.) The site will show you how to tie several classic scarf knots. Brilliant.

Etsy.com

This Web site has a little bit of everything. It's really great for accessories, and it's all handmade. My favorite thing about the site is that you can search for merchandise by color.

GirlPROPS.com

Absolutely phenomenal costume jewelry, hair accessories, and more. Everything is very inexpensive and they have an enormous selection. If you're in Manhattan, visit their Soho store.

Supermaggie.com

This indie designer is based in Louisiana, but her merchandise is carried in boutiques across the country. Her hand-felted scarves and flower pins are phenomenal. The colors are absolutely beautiful. Each one is a work of art.

CarolsDaughter.com

I remember when the first Carol's Daughter store opened in Fort Green, Brooklyn. It was one of those delightful treasures that only a few people knew about. Not for long, though. Their products remain buzzworthy: all-natural skin, hair, makeup, and bath products with an African-American focus. They have the best hair masks and the most delicious fragrances. I'm obsessed with Carol's Ocean Body and Bath Oil.

Kiehl's

Established in 1851 (I know—amazing), Kiehl's creates skincare and beauty products made from natural ingredients—and they're so luxurious. I love, love, love the free samples.

Ricky's

It's so much fun to shop for makeup here. They have a spectacular selection of beauty and hair care products and accessories. A little of everything. And they have lots of fun travel size products so you can find the perfect luxurious shampoo and conditioner. You can shop online, too, but nothing beats the in-store experience.

Sephora

I don't have to tell you: Sephora has the best selection of cosmetics and fragrance in one place that I've ever seen. I especially love all the gift sets and palettes.

STYLE, STYLE, STYLE

Coutorture.com

The name says it all. It's an online style community you *absolutely* must visit.

ChristianvSiriano.com

He won season four of *Project Runway*, and his beautiful clothes are a testament to our good judgment.

Fashiondig.com

This is an online community, retail venue, and blog about everything vintage. So informative, so fabulous.

Fashionista.com

This site is filled with gossip, style commentary, and fashion news. It's a guilty pleasure.

FashionSpace.com

You must check out the indie designers on this international e-commerce site. Of course, they also have a blog.

FrockNYC.com

Gorgeous, gorgeous, gorgeous vintage from the '60s through the '80s. These frocks are not cheap, but each one is a work of art.

Kaboodle.com

A style and design online community that's fun and fresh. Check out the style boards created by other users, or make your own. It's also great for getting ideas and finding new designers.

MichaelKors.com

Need I say more? The man's a genius.

My-Wardrobe.com

You can find high-end shopping and style guides here. They offer a fabulous London-based twist on fashion.

Refinery29.com

A fabulous site for independent style. They have sample sale listings, a blog, and the latest trends from the runway to the street.

TheSartorialist.com
Reviewing street fashion with a couture eye, you will marvel at Scott Shuman's myriad of ideas. His amazing view of the smashing ensembles people are wearing all over the world is not to be missed.

StyleByAli.com
Sample sale listings, regular sale listings, a blog, and fashion, fashion, fashion. It's all here.

StyleHive.com
This young, hip design and pop culture social network is the perfect place to look for the next hot trend.

StyleWillSaveUs.com
It really will! Cutting-edge style commentary through an eco-friendly lens can be found here. Leave it to the English yet again!

WhoWhatWear.com
This site is the cherry on your style sundae. Their blog has all of the celebrity style gossip and commentary you could want. It's completely decadent frivolity.

WornThrough.com
The commentary on style and fashion here may strike you as a little academic, but I find it so interesting.

HOW-TO

bbb.org/us/donating-used-clothes-and-household-items
Again, the name pretty much says it all. The Better Business Bureau posts guidelines for donating clothing here along with information about how to report donations on your tax return.

bbc.co.uk/thread/twiggysfrockexchange
Everything you need to know about how to throw a swap party can be found here. You can even download a kit! It's all about green fashion. Be sure to check out the video tutorials on revamping old garments. The demonstrations are amazingly easy and so fashion-forward.

ehow.com
Exactly what it sounds like: This site features instructions for how to do just about anything. Since anyone can contribute, take its hints with a grain of salt.

SSIA.info
This is the official site of the Shoe Services Institute of America. Who knew? Literally everything you ever wanted to know about shoe care is here. Everything.

EVERYTHING ELSE

BeatMyPrice.com
A branch of RetailMeNot.com, this site allows users to submit the lowest price they've found for a particular item. Economizing takes teamwork, and this site gathers and utilizes pricing information.

Bizrate.com
Go here to compare prices on most name-brand items.

RetailMeNot.com
Find coupons and discount codes for anything you can imagine. Always check this site before making an online purchase.

Shopzilla.com
This site offers another way to comparison shop.

Thefind.com
If there's something you can't find, be sure to look here. Search for products, sales, and so much more.

ThePurpleBook.com

This site helps point you in the direction of the best online shopping. You can search by genre, location, keyword, etc. Great staff reviews and user ratings.

Yelp.com

If you're planning a vacation or just a shopping trip, this Web site has a lot of helpful information. Read a few of the user reviews on any given good or service before you head out. It's such good stuff.

Acknowledgments

ALTHOUGH WRITING A BOOK can at times be a lonely process, publishing a book is a team effort. I am so lucky to have one of the best teams an author could ever hope to work with.

My family and close friends are my bedrock, and as I've written on many occasions, being surrounded by some of the most talented people in the world is the purest form of inspiration anyone could ever have. I know I'm lucky, and I never take these amazing people for granted.

Ruben Toledo is a magician. Through his illustrations, he creates an entire universe of color and form. Again, I'm honored to work with him the way I do. Both he and his wife Isabel have given me (and the world) so very, very much.

What can I say about Rene Alegria but that he makes things happen. Out of nowhere. His ideas continue to gush into the world, as does his humor. His belief in me from the moment I met him allows me to simultaneously soar and keeps me grounded. Together, we're madness, in the best possible way.

The best that RISD has to offer, Vanessa Binder's eye for detail and research helped better this book in so many ways. Nothing gets by her without a comment. Everyone needs someone like her on their team.

Shubhani Sarkar again worked her skills into yet another piece of art through her design. I can't thank her enough. So too did Amy Vreeland and her making sure every word is right on the mark.

Everyone at HarperCollins for their incredible support and enthusiasm. Being a part of the new It! Books imprint gives me great pride. In particular, Hope Innelli, Carrie Kania, Susan Kosko, Kim Lewis, Lorie Pagnozzi, Kevin Callahan, Michael Barrs, Teresa Brady, and Andrea Rosen, among so many others.

Everyone at *Project Runway*, the Weinstein Company, and Lifetime. Your support means everything to me.

The crew at *Marie Claire*, especially Susan Plagemann and Joanna Coles, for embracing me they way they have. Also, to Christina Saratsis, for following up and keeping everything on track.

Finally, to Lucas and David. Nothing happens in my life without my consciously or subconsciously thinking of you. You both are everything to me.